D0569586

Believing and Belonging

A. E. Harvey

Believing and Belonging

The Practice of Believing
in the Church

First published in Great Britain 1984
SPCK
Holy Trinity Church
Marylebone Road
London NW1 4DU

Copyright © A.E. Harvey 1984

All rights reserved. No part of this book may be reproduced or
transmitted in any form or by any means, electronic or
mechanical, including photocopying, recording or by any
information, storage and retrieval system, without permission in
writing from the publisher.

British Library Cataloguing in Publication Data

Harvey, A.E.
    Believing and belonging
    1. Church of England—Doctrines
    I. Title
    230'.3   BX5131.2

    ISBN 0-281-04106-7

Typeset by Academic Typesetting, Gerrards Cross
Printed in Great Britain by
the Chanctonbury Press Limited, Bradford

Contents

Preface

In 1981 the Church of England Doctrine Commission published its Report entitled *Believing in the Church*. This is a book of over three hundred pages, containing essays on a wide variety of topics, and presenting arguments which are often of a technical kind and make considerable demands on the reader. It represents, I believe, an important advance in the thinking of the Church of England about itself, and clarifies many of the questions which are raised by any statement beginning, 'The Church believes. . . ' . But it was deliberately addressed to the more articulate and reflective members of the Church. A book of this size and complexity could hardly be commended for study in parishes throughout the Church of England.

I was a member of the Doctrine Commission throughout the time that it was working on *Believing in the Church*, and came to believe that the ideas we were exploring were of considerable importance for understanding the *doctrinal* importance of many of the activities in which ordinary church members are engaged. I have therefore thought it worth while to try to interest a wider public in the argument by presenting it, not only in a simpler and shorter form, but (in a sense) the other way round. Instead of asking (as the Report did) how specific beliefs have come to be formed in the Church of England, I have started with the individual church member and explored the ways in which someone who actively 'belongs' to the church may come to have an influence on what the church 'believes'. My hope is that I may help my readers to come to see (as I have) some of their routine church activities in a new and encouraging light.

I have drawn constantly on *Believing in the Church* and am grateful to its authors for allowing me to do so. Some of them read part of this book in draft and generously helped me to improve it. I have followed the topics through in roughly the same order, so that it will not be difficult for any reader to find my sources. But I have deliberately refrained from giving frequent references. This is not an introduction or guide to *Believing in the Church*. It is my own extremely personal interpretation of insights I gained from that work. The weaknesses and failings of this book must in no way be attributed to that one. But I hope that all who find something of help and interest in mine will be encouraged to read *Believing in the Church* for themselves, where they will find in purer form most of the ideas which I have here exploited to furnish a presentation which is entirely my own.

Westminster Abbey   A.E.H.
January 1984

1
Believing

The Church of England, along with all the other great churches of the West, has recently been revising and modernizing its forms of public worship. The various revisions have aroused intense discussion and controversy. Fierce objection has been raised to the use of contemporary English, to alleged changes in doctrine that are implicit in the new services, and to the new pattern and ethos of worship which they have encouraged. But one change of great significance has been made which has excited remarkably little comment. Along with the majority of English-speaking churches throughout the world we have quietly moved from the individual to the corporate. When we recite the creed in the Communion service, our new service-books require us to say, not 'I believe', but 'We believe'.

This is not a total innovation. When the original version of what we call the Nicene Creed was promulgated by the assembled bishops at the Council of Nicaea in 325 AD, it took the form of a series of clauses introduced by the phrase, 'We believe'. It was in fact a conciliar statement, that is, a claim by the representatives of the universal Church to have agreed upon what it is that we all believe. But in fact this new creed was a modification of an earlier creed which took its origin in quite different circumstances. For at least a century before the Council of Nicaea, any converts presenting themselves for baptism were challenged with questions asking them whether they believed the fundamental articles of the Christian faith, and replied to each question, 'I believe'. Out of this (it is usually thought) grew a single consecutive profession of belief, introduced by

1

'I believe', and it was this form of profession which was adopted into the worship of the Church from the sixth century onwards. Until very recently, therefore, Christians throughout the world have been accustomed to recite their faith in this apparently individualistic form: 'I believe in one God . . . I believe . . . I believe'. Indeed, Anglicans have done this more than most, since the Book of Common Prayer gives greater prominence to the creeds in worship than they have had in any other church.

The new services, therefore, by changing 'I believe' to 'We believe', have deliberately broken with a very long tradition. The international and interdenominational commission which introduced the change has not published its reasons for doing so. But the fact that the change has been accepted so easily suggests that it is felt by most Christians today to represent a more appropriate way of making a common affirmation. One almost universal feature of modern church life is a greater 'togetherness'. Many Christians (particularly, perhaps, members of the Church of England) used to go to church in a highly private and individual way. Public worship was very much an affair of the individual coming to terms with God in his own conscience and his own understanding, and the fact that members of the congregation often tried to sit as far apart from each other as possible and showed no inclination to greet each other before or after the service was not felt to be scandalous or even surprising. But now, in most English parish churches, the atmosphere is very different. Members of a congregation participate more in worship, are more sensitive to each other's needs and preferences, and for the most part are quite ready to give each other a 'sign of peace' in the form of a handshake. This greater sense of 'togetherness' in church makes it natural that the moment when we make our common profession of faith should be (like the intercessions and the confession of sins) expressed in the first person plural: no longer 'I believe', but 'We believe'.

This change, then, may be in part no more than a reflection of a growing sense of human solidarity, not only among church members, but in society at large. But it is also a sign of a change in our understanding of truth itself. Until recently, most of us have tended to think of truth, knowledge and belief in a very individualistic way. The philosophical tradition of the West has taught us to think of our minds as a blank sheet of paper, which each of us fills up in our own way, imprinting certain pieces of knowledge upon it. We have been taught to think in terms of subject and object: I, the subject, stand over against the world of objects; and when my own judgement corresponds with that which 'really is', then I know the truth. Indeed, one of the consequences of a philosophical tradition which goes right back to Plato has been that we instinctively contrast the *opinion* of the multitude, which is based only on the perceived appearance of things, with the *knowledge* of the individual expert or philosopher, whose intellectual equipment enables him to penetrate the world of appearances and have a glimpse of the truth. In this tradition, what the individual believes is of primary importance; and in religious matters the question of belief is instinctively phrased in individual terms: What do I believe? What do you believe?

Yet, despite this highly individualist approach to knowledge and belief, most of us would recognize that in our day-to-day lives we rely, not only on painstakingly acquired personal knowledge, but also (indeed perhaps more so) on 'common sense', that is, on a wisdom which is essentially *shared.* A recognition of the importance of this corporate (as opposed to individual) form of knowledge has recently made its appearance in philosophy; and indeed the dependence of every individual upon the shared assumptions and shared wisdom of the society in which he lives is a presupposition of a whole new scholarly discipline known as 'sociology of knowledge'. We know what we know, not (for the most part) because we have individually chosen to know precisely this and not something else, but because we belong to a society which accepts certain forms of education and communication; and if we study society from this point of view, we begin to realize the enormous influence which it exerts upon the cognitive powers of any individual. What he knows by his own choice and questioning is relatively small. What he knows as a member of society is very much greater.

It is not only the content of our knowledge which is socially conditioned. The form in which we grasp it and express it is also something which we share with others. Intensive study has been devoted in recent years to the influence of the language we speak upon our thoughts and concepts. To put the matter crudely: it is impossible to think anything (or at least to know precisely what we are thinking) unless we can put it into words; and the pattern of our language places limits on the kinds of thoughts we can have. Of course, both poets and scientists may reach out to ideas and concepts which have never been expressed before and by so doing may extend the possibilities of language; but for the most part any progress which each of us may make in acquiring knowledge is conditioned by the resources of the language we use to express it. This language is our shared inheritance; and it ensures that the knowledge that any of us acquires bears a close relationship to that of others who speak the same language.

Even in science, there has been a growing recognition of the influence of the community on the research of the individual. It is natural to think of science as essentially a procedure for amassing information about the physical world. Science, we believe, is concerned with 'hard facts', facts which are 'out there', waiting to be discovered by the scientist. But philosophers of science have been coming to realize that this is not how science in fact advances. Scientists are confronted, like anyone else, with a bewildering mass of apparently unrelated phenomena. To understand what they observe, they bring forward some framework or model which seems to make sense of the phenomena so far observed. Further observations may confirm their hypothesis; or they may cause them to modify the framework, or even abandon it altogether. But without the framework they could make little progress. Their knowledge is not primarily the product of individual observation but of a shared approach to the observable world. A scientist may say, 'I personally believe that the structure of this molecule is such and such'; and he may have means of verifying his belief. But it is not a belief which he could ever have entertained had he not been nurtured in a community of scientists who all believe in the molecular structure of matter. A scientist must say 'We believe' far more often than he says 'I believe'.

But is this true also of religious belief? It is natural to think of religion as a highly personal and private matter —'what a man does with his solitude', in A.N. Whitehead's phrase; and in the long run, however much I may identify myself with a group or society of other people all professing the same faith, it is my own personal relationship with God, my own salvation, which is at stake. But to say this is to suppose that I am really free to choose the religious beliefs which I hold; and of course this is true, in the sense that I am free to weigh up the arguments for and against, free to join a church or leave it, free to form my own judgement on matters of Christian faith and morals. Yet in another sense I

5

am certainly not free. Whether or not I believe in God is likely to depend on many factors outside my control. My upbringing, my social background, my profession and my circle of acquaintance will certainly exert pressure on me one way or the other, and the less I am aware of this pressure the more I deceive myself if I assume that my religious convictions are the result of an altogether free choice. Sociological study has confirmed the impression, which can be obtained by simple observation, that Christian belief and practice tend to go with particular social environments, professions and even politics. To put it crudely, you are much more likely to be a believer if you are a member of the professional classes, live in a prosperous suburb and have somewhat conservative political views than if you are a manual worker in East London. This does not mean, of course, that you cannot freely accept or deny the truth of Christianity wherever you are; but it does mean that external factors of this kind must have a considerable influence, of which you may or may not be conscious, on your decision. It also means that if you are a member of a church you are likely to be there, at least in part, because you share the background and attitudes of others.

There is of course a perfectly proper reaction to what has just been said: one may immediately feel challenged to assert one's own individuality. The more I am told that I behave as I would be expected to behave as a member of a particular class or group, the more emphatically I may try to assert my independence; and in matters of religion I am surely at least as free to swim against the tide as I am in matters of social convention or choice of career. But there is another rather more fundamental reason why the religious faith of most of us is by no means an individual possession. If I am asked to give an account of what I believe, I may find it difficult, if not impossible, to give a satisfactory answer. There may be certain questions, or 'matters of principle', on which I have clear convictions, and these I can state in definite terms. But they will not themselves add up to a system of belief or a complete world-view. If I am honest, I shall have to admit that my opinions, my moral decisions and my religious practice all depend upon a large number of assumptions and attitudes of which I may be almost unconscious and which I would find it difficult to express adequately in words. And these deeper assumptions and attitudes are not ones which, for the most part, I have consciously and deliberately chosen for myself. They are ones which I have inherited from my family upbringing, absorbed in the course of my education, and slowly adopted as un-questioned guidelines for life. These all form a part of my total belief. They are mine, but I share them with all those from whom, consciously or unconsciously, I have adopted them. In this sense also, it may be appropriate to say 'We believe' rather than 'I believe'.

The convinced individualist may still not be satisfied. No matter, he may say, where I got my beliefs from; no matter what influences of class or upbringing I may have been exposed to; no matter even that I share the language and concepts in which my beliefs are expressed with countless others – my beliefs are still my own, I am free to hold them or discard them, to articulate and account for them, just as I choose. My religious faith is a matter of 'I believe'; 'we believe' is inappropriate.

So long as the individualist is an outsider and speaks entirely for himself, this protest is surely justified; and indeed a long tradition of Christian theological writing has taken it for granted that this is in fact the situation of any individual confronted with the necessity to make a personal decision for or against the Christian faith. The report of the previous Doctrine Commission, for example, was written in almost entirely individualistic terms, and, under the title *Christian Believing*, sought to grapple with the problems an individual may have today as he tries to come to terms with the historic formulations of Christian belief. But in fact such an enquirer is by no means typical. It is not often that an individual approaches questions of religious faith with a completely open and uncluttered mind. He will already have been influenced, consciously or unconsciously, by a large number of attitudes, experiences and preferences; and his ultimate decision may be determined as much by these as by the arguments which he is consciously weighing at the time. It would be a mistake to imagine that coming to accept the Christian faith is like learning a foreign language or the rules of chess, as if one were gradually advancing from one piece of knowledge to another until one could finally say, 'I know it all'.

Consider, for instance, how one decides to identify oneself with a political party. Normally, one is attracted by certain claims or promises made by that party; or one likes some of its attitudes or assumptions; or one may just warm personally to some of its members. One then may join. Thereafter, one gradually learns more of the party's policies and absorbs more of its philosophy and aspirations. Unless one actually comes to regret one's decision and leaves the party, one will continue to discover gradually the implications of belonging, and will allow the party's political principles to influence one's own thinking. Indeed, on many matters one will probably take the party's policy on trust; one can't know about everything, and one simply assumes that the party's view on some matters will be in accordance with its known policy on others. One is still of course free to criticize or reject certain doctrines or policies, though these will probably have to be fairly minor ones if one is to remain a loyal member of the party. But it is surely true of most people that to say, 'I am a Conservative', or 'I am a Socialist', does not imply that they are familiar with every aspect of their chosen party's thinking and policy. Certain things have influenced them to declare their allegiance; the rest they are prepared, at least for the time being, to take on trust.

The situation of someone who decides to join a church is in many ways very similar. Such a person does not normally go through a long process of investigation, checking the results of his own thinking against what he believes to be the official teaching of the church, and then, when he finds it matches all the way along, finally making his decision. He is normally persuaded to belong on the basis of a relatively small number of factors: his acceptance of certain fundamental Christian doctrines, his personal admiration of other Christians, or even just a willingness to conform to the religious views and practices of his acquaintances. But from then on he will find his belief and conduct are being gradually formed and strengthened by the institution to which he has declared his allegiance. This does not mean (at least in the major Christian churches, whatever may be true in certain highly authoritarian sects) that he must accept uncritically everything he is told. He is positively encouraged to seek and appropriate the truth for himself, and it is always possible that his doubts and difficulties may become such that he has to suspend belief or even leave the church. But in the meantime he does not refuse to say the creed alongside his fellow-members of the church, just because he has not yet made up his mind about every clause. To say the creed is rather to express solidarity with the church whose doctrines and attitudes he is still exploring. Hence, 'We believe' may be at least as appropriate as 'I believe'.

This description of religious commitment may be tested by asking oneself what one would actually reply to a questioner who wanted to know what one's religious beliefs are. Certain things a Christian would probably say without much hesitation; that he believes there is a God; that the Bible is (in some sense) true; that our sins are forgiven; and so forth. But if he were pressed to give a comprehensive and coherent account of his beliefs, he would probably find it impossible to do so. Indeed, the more he thought about it the more he would probably be dismayed to realize that a great deal of what he claims to believe consists of assumptions and attitudes which he has never searchingly examined or consciously made his own, and which, even when he has reflected upon it, he finds it difficult to articulate coherently. He probably has to admit that he takes a great deal on trust from the church and from Christian tradition. To a great extent what he believes himself is what the church believes.

This is not to say by any means that a Christian believes only what the church believes, or that what any individual member of the church believes is necessarily identical with official church doctrine. In all these matters, the relationship of the individual to the corporate institution is much more complicated than that – indeed to elucidate this relationship will be one of the tasks of this book. But it does seem to follow that the church's belief will have considerable influence on the belief of the individual. There are parts of the Christian faith which one may hold with deep personal conviction, which one may have no difficulty in expressing in one's own words, and which one knows one shares with other Christians. But there are bound to be other parts about which one is less clear and certain and which, to a greater or lesser extent, one takes on trust. Even beliefs which one feels to be most clear, certain and personal

10

owe much of both their content and formulation to the language, culture and religious tradition of those with whom one shares them. It seems one can hardly give an account of one's own personal faith without acknowledging some debt to the belief of the church.

But what does the church believe? Until we can ascertain that, it seems we cannot get much further in discovering what we do or ought to believe ourselves. And it is therefore extremely frustrating when theologians say (as they seem so often to say) that there is no simple answer to this question either. Indeed, when *Believing in the Church* was published, one of the main criticisms levelled against it was that it completely failed to meet the need which so many people feel to know what it is that the church now believes. Surely there is a danger (in view of all that has been said so far) that if the church is found to speak with as uncertain a voice as the individual we may none of us be able to say where we stand at all.

But before we join this chorus of disappointment we need to be sure what it is we are asking for. 'The Church believes' is a curious expression. How can an organization or society be said to 'believe' something? Take once again the example of a political party. A politician may well say, 'This party believes. . . ' . But how is one to establish just what these beliefs are? One may read the party's election manifesto; one may talk to one's M.P.; one may study the writings and memoirs of former leaders of the party; one may go to local constituency meetings. None of these sources of information will yield exactly the same answer as any other. For a complete answer they must all be taken into account, and even then there is an element of the provisional. The party's beliefs are formed and influenced by countless individuals, and that influence is still at work. One's analysis of the party's beliefs may be out of

11

date as soon as it is completed – may even, if it is widely circulated, be itself one of the causes of change.

Once again, we must not apply the analogy too strictly. There are important differences between the church and a political party, not least the fact that the church claims to possess the *truth* as revealed by God, whereas a political party can proclaim at most an opinion, an option and a policy. Nevertheless, it would be a mistake to assume that there is nothing in common between the two. Certainly, the church is entrusted with divine truth, and part of its function is to preserve this truth and impart it to successive generations of Christians. In this sense, the church is a 'teaching church', *ecclesia docens*, and its members are necessarily for ever learners. But even in the Roman Catholic Church, where this principle has been extremely influential, it does not follow that the belief of the church can simply be read off from the pronouncements of its teachers. All teaching, if it is to convey the truth, must awaken a response; and that response (or lack of it) will in turn affect all subsequent teaching. Indeed it is as true of a church as of a political party that there is no single source from which the church's belief can be discovered. If the phrase, 'the church believes', has any meaning (which it surely does), then this meaning must be discovered in the complex interplay between the personal belief of the individual and the corporate believing of the church. It is not only (as we have seen) that the individual's belief is in many respects dependent on the church's belief. It is also true that what the church believes is to a certain extent affected by what its individual members believe. Indeed individual Christians carry as heavy and challenging a responsibility for the belief of the church as they do for its standard of conduct. It is this responsibility and this challenge – so little realized by Christians today – which is the subject of the following chapters.

2
Exploring

One of the very first things a member of the church is required to do is to read the Bible. This seems reasonable: any organization is likely to have some required reading for its members – a book of rules, a history of the society, a statement of aims and principles. There is nothing surprising in the church making a similar demand.

But the Bible is singularly unlike any literature which an organization would normally think of placing in the hands of its members. It is (by comparison) extremely long; and the greater part of it (the Old Testament) is explicitly stated by Christians to be obsolete, even though they claim that it remains somehow helpful and even necessary reading. It is a collection of varied writings, which are far from self-explanatory, and display no clear principle of arrangement. Moreover, it seems to have to be treated in a special way. In the past, this was emphasized by soft leather bindings, fine printing on thin paper, two columns to a page – all features which tended to make it seem different from any other book. Recently, there has been a move in the other direction: the Bible has been published in paperback, there have been modern translations, the format is often contemporary, even catchy. Yet however much we are urged to read the Bible 'like any other book', it remains strangely *unlike* other books. There is still a reluctance to publish it with the kind of aids to the reader which any comparable book would normally provide – an index, explanatory footnotes, clear divisions between different kinds of writing, even an intelligible table of contents. It is clear that, whatever comparisons may be made with other writings (even ones which come down, as the Bible does, from a culture which existed two or three thousand years ago), the Bible continues to be regarded as a special – indeed unique – book, and so has to be read in a special way.

How does a Christian learn this 'special way'? It is clearly not enough to be told that it contains the truth about God, and that one must therefore take it more seriously than any other book. One may open it at Leviticus, and find a series of regulations about clean and unclean foods which have no possible relevance to the life of a Christian today; one may go to the beginning of the New Testament, and be confronted with the genealogy on the first page of Matthew's Gospel – a long list of exotic-sounding names; one may boldly start on a letter of St Paul, only to find that it appears to be concerned with issues (such as circumcision, or mysterious heresies) which seem both obscure and remote from the modern world. At the very least it will be necessary to have some guidance to find one's way about. But more than that: one may readily grant that some parts of the Bible, such as the Gospels or certain passages of Old Testament prophecy, often speak very directly to the reader, even today. In particular, the person and message of Jesus continue to make an immediate impact on many people. Yet even the most easily intelligible parts of his teaching demand considerable interpretation if they are to be taken seriously as a basis for conduct and faith. Sometimes his demands are such that they seem impossible to fulfil at all; sometimes they presuppose social and cultural conditions totally different from our own; sometimes they seem only to sharpen the moral dilemmas we already find ouselves in. To extract from them a standard of personal behaviour, let alone a charter for the existence of the Church, is a task which one could not

14

hope to perform without seeking assistance.

But who should provide this assistance? A different kind of answer may be given in different parts of the Church. In the Roman Catholic Church it has always been affirmed that the faithful must understand Scripture in the light of the interpretation offered by the Church. It was the Church, after all, which first determined which of the allegedly 'apostolic' writings which were circulating in the early centuries should be included in the canon of holy Scripture; it was the great councils which defined the Christian doctrines which could legitimately be inferred from Scripture; and on countless other matters it has necessarily been the Church which has guided the judgement of the believer through a long and carefully controlled tradition of interpretation. Today, it is true, the Roman Catholic believer, who in the past had little direct access to the Scriptures, is actively encouraged to read them; but he is still expected to use guides and commentaries which pay full attention to the Catholic tradition of biblical interpretation.

Protestant Christianity has always reacted sharply against this view. The Bible is the word of God, and speaks directly and personally to every human being who opens his heart and mind to it. It is surely wrong to suggest that the mediation and control of the Church is necessary, or even desirable. Consequently the characteristic style of Bible study for both individuals and groups in Protestant churches has been one that promises a direct confrontation between the believer and the divine message addressed to him in the pages of Scripture. Any appeal to 'tradition' is regarded as an evasion.

Yet this determination to enter into direct and personal converse with the inspired truth as revealed in Scripture does not do away with the difficulties referred to earlier. Despite the many passages which seem luminously clear and direct, the Bible as a whole remains obscure and confusing unless some guidance is given. It is hardly sufficient to affirm, as Calvin did, that the Holy Spirit will reveal its meaning to the sincere believer: the Holy Spirit must be expected to make use of human agents of elucidation. Nor is it sufficient to say, with Luther, that serious attention need be given only to those passages which manifestly 'proclaim Christ'. To discern precisely which these passages are, and what their meaning is, is a task beyond the capacity of most laymen. Accordingly every evangelical Bible study group, however committed it may be to personal, honest and unmediated attention to the word of God, will have recourse to its leader for guidance on many matters of interpretation; the leader, in turn, will have learnt from others; and behind it all, for ultimate reference, there will be a series of commentaries, all by authors known and approved within evangelical circles, whose style of interpretation constitutes a veritable 'tradition'.

So far we have been trying to establish what is the 'special way' in which Christians may be expected to read the Bible. We have suggested that the sheer difficulty and obscurity of these writings, which come to us from a culture and a period of history at such a distance from our own, make it inevitable that the reader should need expert help if he is to make sense of them; and we have observed that, in one form or another, this help is likely to be provided through the church. But it would be a great mistake to think that it is only or even mainly the difficulty of the Bible which causes the problem. The real questions begin to emerge when we look more closely at the Bible itself and at the use which is actually made of it by Christians. We began by comparing it to a rule book or standard work of reference which any organization might put in the hands of its members to guide their thinking and conduct. To a certain extent this comparison is apt, in that Christians do in fact consult their Bibles in order to decide what they should think and do. But the comparison also brings out a very important difference. Rule books, constitutions and foundation documents are normally written for this very purpose: they set out principles and regulations, objectives and accepted practices, admonition and exhortation, appropriate to the effective running of the society. Now it is true that the Bible does contain material of this kind. There are laws and exhortations, there are principles and admonitions, there are statements about the character and purposes of the church. But it must immediately be said that this is not the only kind of material contained in holy Scripture, or even its most characteristic. There is myth and poetry, there is prophecy and ecstatic vision; above all, there is narrative. Far the greater part of the Bible consists of stories of one kind or another. There is the overarching story, mythological in scale, of the beginning and end of the created world; there is a long succession of apparently historical narratives recording the vicissitudes of ancient Israel, narratives which also provide the necessary context for understanding the poetical utterances of the great Hebrew prophets; there is the early history of the Church as related in Acts; and even the teaching of Jesus, though it is occasionally concentrated in set pieces such as the Sermon on the Mount or the Farewell Discourses, is always set in the context of the story of his life and is indeed subservient to it. It was not for a century after the writing of the New Testament Gospels that any attempt was made to compile the teaching of Jesus independently of its narrative framework – and then it was done by heretical teachers outside the community of orthodox Christian faith. And it was many centuries later before, in a book such as *The Imitation of Christ*, the essence of Christ's teaching was deliberately presented thematically with no attempt to set it in the context of his earthly ministry.

If one is asked, therefore, what is the characteristic mode of biblical writing, one will have to admit that it is not legal or exhortatory or even (in the normal sense of the word as applied to literature) 'religious': it is narrative. And this means that the purpose for which it is studied by Christians cannot be so easily inferred from it as would be the case, say, with the rule book of a club. Christians may certainly expect that by reading the Bible they will learn more of the nature of God and of his demands upon us. But it will be only rarely that the Bible will be able to give them straight answers to their questions. Sometimes, it is true, there may be a piece of teaching in it which has direct application even to people of today; the Ten Commandments, for instance, are often said to be of timeless validity, though, being mainly prohibitions rather than positive directions, they are quite insufficient to provide the basis of a moral code. It is also true that many people are encouraged to think that the Bible does offer immediate and consistent guidance for prayer, thought and action: much traditional Bible-study literature seeks to distil a 'thought for the day', a prayer, or a personal resolution, out of almost every verse of Scripture. But the difficulty of doing this is not just that so many things have changed since the Scriptures were written that there is no direct route from an instruction given, say, by St Paul to his converts in Corinth to the answer to a social problem of today. It is rather that the greater part of Scripture is in any case quite inappropriate to answering such questions at all. It is narrative; and there is no direct route from the story of what someone said or did on a particular occasion to what I should do or say at this moment. Even Jesus' parables, which are stories deliberately told as a means of teaching, are not capable of being neatly applied to modern circumstances; rather, they challenge their hearers to re-examine their presuppositions, or to look at themselves in a new light.

Our problem with the Bible, therefore, is a far more complex and searching one than its mere strangeness and datedness. It is rather that, to answer questions about what we should believe (doctrine) or how we should behave (morals), it is simply inappropriate. What we need is statements about God, or instructions about living; what we are offered, again and again, is a story. We must not oversimplify. These stories contain much besides mere narrative. They often include substantial quantities of teaching and exhortation. But even if one deliberately collects and tries to arrange this material (a task undertaken again and again by theologians), not only is it difficult to construct a consistent system of doctrine or ethics out of it (which is why it is attempted again and again by theologians), but the enterprise itself does not seem to be doing justice to the real content of the Bible. Ultimately, our faith depends not on certain abstract statements about God (such as that he is just and merciful) but on certain specific acts which we believe him to have performed: God created man, entered into a covenant relationship with him, sent his Son to redeem him and so forth. These affirmations are specific, and are in the past tense. They are part of a narrative. And it is this which Christians have to come to terms with if they are to grasp their salvation and to continue as active members of the Church.

All this makes the Bible look very unlike the kind of literature which an organization would normally place in the hands of its members to guide their thinking and conduct. Indeed we have to take the question one stage further back and ask why Christians in fact go on reading it at all. Would it not be far easier, and far more conducive to harmonious and effective church life, to produce a compendium of Christian teaching on faith and morals which we could all refer to whenever we were in doubt about our beliefs or our duties?

This is in fact not a new idea at all. From very early times the Church possessed some form of a 'creed', which embodied the fundamental Christian doctrines; and it was not long before it also devised 'catechisms', that is, concise summaries of Christian faith and morals suitable for the use of recent converts. Indeed for many centuries the Church in both East and West did little to encourage ordinary lay people to read the Bible, regarding it as both safer and more effective to provide summaries and directives issued by competent church authorities. This became in time one of the principal issues of the Reformation, which brought to a head a widespread protest against the denial of free access to the Scriptures to the laity at large. This in turn was more than just a protest against the misuse of the Church's authority. It was a recognition of a quality inherent in the Bible itself. Creeds, catechisms and all other official formulations of Christian belief and practice are ultimately derived from Scripture. But this is not to say that they can ever replace Scripture. As we have seen, Scripture is not such as to lend itself to being summarized and systematized. Anyone who attempts to do so (and in every generation there are theologians who make the attempt as a contribution to the intellectual and spiritual life of the Church) has to make countless judgements on what to put in and what to leave out, what to emphasize and what to pass over, how to understand some passages, how to work out the implications of others. Each of these judgements can be challenged by others – and always for the same reason: that it is not faithful, or does not do justice, to what anyone can read for himself in the Bible. It is this inevitable inadequacy and provisionality of every system of church teaching which lies behind the great Reformation principle that the Church stands always beneath the judgement of Scripture. But there is also a still more fundamental reason. The narrative quality of Scripture is not a kind of unfortunate accident which creeds, catechisms and theological treatises are intended to rectify. It is its most characteristic element; one might almost say its genius. It is indeed this which has assured the continued vitality of the Bible in the Church down the ages, long after more formal and prosaic formulations of belief would have been relegated to the library or the museum.

We therefore have to return to our question, why Christians continue to read the Bible and what they expect to gain from it, recognizing that there will not be as simple an answer to it as there would be in the case of a set of rules or principles. Much of the Bible is story; and perhaps we can get some help if we consider for a moment why we attend to certain other stories. The stories we listen to in childhood are significant from this point of view. We have all had some favourite story which we liked to have told to us again and again; not (usually) because it was the most sensational of the ones we knew (indeed the initial thrill of suspense does not survive frequent repetition), or the most brilliantly told, or the most exotic or imaginative; but because we in some way identified with it, were caught up in it, and reassured or inspired by it. And so it is with stories which continue to work upon us in adult life. They tell us something important about the world and about ourselves. Each time we hear them they exercise some influence on us, indeed they positively require retelling from time to time. They become, in a sense, 'our' stories.

The analogy with the Bible is illuminating. It helps us to see, for instance, why Scripture cannot be treated like a text-book, to be learnt and absorbed until it is of no further use. (Possibly it is precisely because it *is* treated like a text-book in so much religious education that it loses its power to influence life.) Like a great story – or rather, like a collection of stories – it has to be read again and again. We shall see in a later chapter that this is borne out in public worship. In church, the Bible is not read as if one were getting through a syllabus of required reading, after which one could go on to something else. Rather, it is the same stories which are constantly attended to, year after year. For they are stories which involve us, challenge us, judge us and inspire us. To put it somewhat crudely, we listen to the story told by the Bible in order to bring the story of our own lives into conformity with it.

There is however another implication of this 'story' aspect of the Bible which brings us back to the question from which we started. When the foundation-literature of a movement or organization consists mainly of rules and precepts (like the Jewish Talmud, for example), it requires experts to expound and interpret it. The beginner has to undertake systematic study and master a mass of material before he can utter an opinion that deserves a hearing. To a certain extent this is true also of the Bible: there are many technical matters which bear upon the meaning of a text, and the work of biblical scholars provides essential guidance in many cases. Yet in the study of the Bible this is not the end of the matter. Bible study is not like learning a textbook or a foreign language. It does not consist in gradually building up more knowledge and expertise. The Bible presents a story; and the appropriate response to that story is not, or certainly is not only, an effort to learn and understand all the relevant facts. It is rather to allow the story to do what all great stories do, that is, to enlarge one's experience, challenge one's convictions, reinforce one's aspirations, stir one's imagination. But further: the story the Bible tells is, in more than one sense, *true*. Reading the Bible involves personally coming to terms with that truth, and fashioning one's thinking, praying and living accordingly. In this, there are no 'experts'. There are only bold explorers and patient followers, restless enquirers and faithful practitioners, saints and sinners – all united in the same conviction that, through Scripture, God continues to give us new knowledge and experience of himself up to the day of our death.

It follows that the study of the Bible can never be only a matter for the individual. Of course there is a place for private Bible study. No amount of emphasis on the social reality of religion affects the fact that God has a profound and intimate relationship with every individual, and one of the ways in which this relationship is awakened and sustained is through the personal study of Scripture. But (as we saw in Chapter 1) it would be a mistake to suppose that any of us can approach this study as an artist approaches a blank sheet of paper, free to make of it what we will. Which passages we find arresting and interesting, what sense we attribute to certain words and expressions, how we find connections between one part and another – all will depend on attitudes, skills and presuppositions we have inherited from others. We shall find that the results of our own personal Bible study are not greatly different from those of others who have received a similar education and have a similar religious background. As we persevere, we shall naturally acknowledge the value of the help which can be given by commentaries, devotional books, preaching and instruction. But the more we receive such help, the harder it is to distinguish between our own personal understanding of the Bible and that which we have received from, and share with, others.

But (it must be said again) the Bible is not like a syllabus that has to be worked through. Its very character, consisting of narrative, poetry, vision, exhortation, prevents it from being studied and learnt 'like any other book'. The object is not just more knowledge, familiarity or expertise. The Bible demands a response. The response each of us makes, though prepared for by the culture, education and experience we share with others, is nevertheless our own; and when we make it, we contribute something of our own to the shared quest for truth that is going on all around us in the church. The appropriate model is not that of students in a class, working away until they know as much as their master: Bible reading is never only, and seldom even predominantly, a pursuit of knowledge. A better model is a team of explorers, some much better trained and more experienced than others, but any of them liable to come across a new discovery which could ultimately affect the team's whole understanding of the region being explored. Consciously or unconsciously, every student of the Bible will for much of the time be following in the footsteps of others; but at any moment he may find a new path which will be of service to those who follow.

The same analogy can tell us something about the function of biblical scholarship. The team must have its experts. Some of them may be like the geologists and botanists who accompany a geographical expedition, making a detailed survey of things the explorers have passed over more rapidly. But some will be expected to be up in front, using their superior knowledge and experience to chart out lines of advance and assess the possibilities and difficulties of the terrain. These experts may make mistakes. They may use their skill to move so much faster than the rest that they lose contact with those following them and so cease to give effective guidance. They may recommend a path which is so precipitous that it is useless to any but those as skilled as themselves. They may even be so misled by their superior skills that they propose a direction which, by sheer common sense, the rest of the team knows to be impractical and refuses to follow. Yet, despite these risks of error and misjudgement, these same experts remain indispensable for the day-to-day progress of the expedition.

In the study of the Bible, the experts are the scholars and the theologians. Sometimes (like the botanists) they work behind the lines, revising texts and translations, and performing quiet and unsensational service to the church. More often they are out in front, testing the way forward. There, they run the risk of failure. They may go too fast, and get out of earshot of those trying to follow (a charge frequently levelled against academics for the obscure and technical character of their writing). They may seem to recommend a course of study which is far too elaborate and recondite for the ordinary lay Christian to be able to follow, and so give the damaging impression that the study of the Bible itself can be undertaken only by experts. They may even try out a scheme of exploration which everyone else senses to be likely to lead nowhere; though they may discover some useful things along the way, they will in due course find that no one is following them – as has happened in the case of more than one school of German exegesis which, when subjected to the judgement of the more pragmatic British student, has turned out to be too theoretical to serve as a guide for Christian Bible study. Yet, despite all these risks, the work of the scholar, even if only as background information, remains indispensable to everyone who is making his own exploration into the Bible.

Let us take, as an example of all this, a particularly

startling instance of the teaching of Jesus: 'Let the dead bury their dead.' The sentence is challenging and suggestive, and may arouse an immediate response: the reader may identify some activity of his own as being 'dead' and ripe for burial, and leave it to others to attend to while he seizes a new opportunity for Christian service. Whether or not this was the original intention of Jesus' pronouncement, we can agree that this would be a case of it continuing to inspire Christian conduct today. But it would be natural also for the reader to seek more expert guidance. Scholars will tell him (either directly through their books, or indirectly through friends or pastors who have read their books) of the paramount importance ascribed in ancient times to the duty of attending to the burial of a close relative. Jesus' saying therefore was more than surprising: it was, if taken literally, quite shocking. But was it to be taken literally? Scholars will remind him (though he could of course have noticed this for himself) that an element of sometimes almost grotesque exaggeration undoubtedly occurs in the teaching of Jesus – a speck of dust in your brother's eye compared with a *beam* or *plank* in your own eye! Moreover they may compare this saying with many others (which again he could have done for himself, given sufficient leisure and observation) which seem to presuppose that Jesus has brought an altogether exceptional situation into human affairs, which justifies exceptional courses of action. The reader may then ask himself what kind of response to this saying would now be appropriate: in what sense can Jesus now address him as if the situation were exceptional, justifying an exceptional course of action? Even allowing for an element of exaggeration in Jesus' saying, what personal sacrifices can he make which would measure up to such a radical challenge? For help, he may turn to the history of the Church, or the lives of the saints, or (most likely) to the

experience of his fellow-Christians in order to get some
idea of a response – say a particular renunciation or
change of life-style – appropriate to his own circumstances; he will then have to decide – and may again
need the encouragement and advice of his fellow-
Christians – whether he can adopt such a course of
action himself. If he does, he will not be acting for himself alone: he will be strengthening the witness of the
whole Church that such a response is the appropriate
one for a Christian to make. Indeed he may be doing
more than that. He may have worked out a response
which is truly appropriate but which had not been ven-
tured by anyone before. By his action he may have
given credibility to a slightly new interpretation of
Jesus' teaching, which, if it stands the test of repetition
by others, may gradually enter the tradition of Christian
response which members of the Church hand on to one
another by writing and teaching, preaching and example.
This complex process of mutual interaction is potentially at work every time a Christian opens the Bible or
takes part in a study group. It may not always be conscious, sometimes it is barely vigorous enough to have
any influence on the course of church life. But the
possibility is always there; and it is this that is meant by
the statement that the study of the Bible is a corporate
activity of the Church.

In fact one can go further. One can say that, in a
sense, it actually *constitutes* the Church. Suppose for a
moment that a particular church or congregation has
given up reading the Bible altogether. Their members,
they say, have heard it long enough; the important bits
they know almost by heart, the rest contains so many
obscurities, oddities and even obscenities that they find
it much better to read something more edifying by a
modern Christian writer – the poems of T.S. Eliot, for
example. What is wrong with this? In some ways this

church may have just as 'good Christians' as any other, and they may in fact have discovered certain dimensions of Christianity which could only be seen through modern literature. But one senses that something is missing. This may not be knowledge; for a considerable time they may remember as much of the Bible as many other church congregations ever know anyway. But what is missing is the exposure to the word of God, the constant wrestling with its meaning, the repeated recital of a story or stories which influence our lives, that absolute commitment to continue the search for the truth of God in those writings in which we believe that he has revealed it. There is a kind of constant attention to the Bible which, in the long run, one can see is essential to the life of the Church. Indeed, if it ceased altogether, it is difficult to see how the Church could continue to exist. Conversely, so long as it does exist, an essential responsibility of all church members is that of participating according to the gifts and capabilities of each – whether by technical scholarship, active lay study or simply by faithful and responsive reading and listening – in that attention and expectancy with which the Scriptures must always be 'read, marked and inwardly digested' in every part of the Church.

3
Saying and Singing

It is often said that the best way to find out what a member of the Church of England believes is to attend a service in a parish church. In church, forms of words are used again and again which imply that the worshippers have certain beliefs. In theory, it ought to be possible to read off from these forms of words what doctrines are being assented to. And in fact the Book of Common Prayer has traditionally been appealed to as one of the ultimate sources for the teaching and beliefs of the Church of England (the others include Scripture, the Creeds, and the Articles of Religion).

In practice it is not so simple – which is just as well for our argument. If it were really the case that what we believe can be read off from what we say in church, then it is difficult to see how the ordinary church member could possibly have any say in the matter. Our forms of prayer are for the most part highly traditional. Many elements in them go back many hundreds of years. From Cranmer's First Prayer Book of 1549 to the Alternative Service Book of 1980, such changes as have been made have been mainly the work of a committee of experts. This is hardly the field in which we would expect the ordinary lay member of a parish congregation to be involved; and if in fact our forms of service determine what we believe, then it seems to follow that most of us can hardly have any responsibility for our beliefs at all. We simply repeat what we read on the pages of the prayer book. But in fact none of this is more than half true. Certainly, our forms of prayer are some guide to what we believe. No church would tolerate a prayer book which consistently forced its members to say things they found incredible or distasteful. And when services are revised or rewritten (as has been happening with some frequency in the Church of England during the last few years), there are usually one or two tell-tale pointers in the wording to particular theological positions which it was felt must be allowed for in our public worship. But this does not mean that the beliefs of each one of us are necessarily represented in any prayer book. The reality is far more complicated.

In the first place, there is the obvious fact that each individual will relate differently to the various forms of prayer which are prescribed. Those that suit us we may join in saying with great conviction; others we may feel less happy with; and there are probably words or sentences in every service that we have never thought carefully about at all. There is perhaps nothing we deeply object to – if there were, we would have to consider, in all honesty, whether we could continue as members of the church. But few of us would want to say that a particular form of service expresses *precisely* what we believe.

In the second place, the kind of language which occurs in a form of service is as difficult to find doctrine in as Scripture is – a great deal of it in fact consists of the recitation or quotation of passages from Scripture. Every now and again a sentence may contain explicit doctrine: 'Who made there, by his one oblation of himself once offered, a full, perfect and sufficient sacrifice' is a clear example. But it is significant that this comes from the central prayer in the Communion service, which is the one over which theologians always wrangle most intensively in any attempt at liturgical revision. Passions still run high over the question whether and how a word such as 'sacrifice' should be used in the course of the Eucharist, or whether a form of intercession is permissible which may be held to imply that prayer may be offered for the souls of the departed. But (whatever may have been the case in the past) it is unlikely that many lay Christians feel that they have a personal stake in these questions: they are thrashed out in committees of experts, or between representatives of church 'parties' in the General Synod, rather than in informed discussion in a parish meeting. Moreover, these heavily charged doctrinal passages are the exception rather than the rule. For the most part the language of worship is that of praise, penitence and petition. It certainly implies beliefs about God and man; but these beliefs are shared by Christians of all denominations, and indeed many of our services (such as marriages or harvest festivals) are joined in quite happily by people with very little conscious faith at all. Few lay members of the church would want to say that their beliefs are determined by what they say or sing in church, or that what they believe can be read off from a prayer book.

But this is not to say that members of the church do not care deeply about the forms of public worship. They may have little direct say, and relatively little interest, in the precise wording of their service books from a doctrinal point of view. But a great many of them are passionately concerned with it from the point of view of style; indeed the controversy which has been raging in the last few years over the preservation and continued use in worship of the Book of Common Prayer has been almost entirely over the question of seventeenth-century versus modern English. That is to say: even if most of us are not greatly concerned about the exact *content* of our worship, we care a great deal about its *style*. And the style depends on far more than the language of the service. It is created by the choice of hymns and the manner of singing; the degree to which

31

members of the congregation participate; the arrangement of seating and furniture in the church; the choice
and character of services. All of these are matters for
which church members have some responsibility; and all
of them say something – some of them say a great deal –
about what church members believe.

A good example is provided by what is probably the
greatest change which has been seen in the worship of
the Church of England in this century: the emergence of
the 'Parish Communion' as the main service in parishes
on Sunday mornings, replacing sung Matins or (in many
Anglo-catholic parishes) High Mass. This change is
widely welcomed by the clergy on theological grounds:
it gives to the Eucharist its rightful place as the central
act of worship of every Christian congregation. Somewhat to their consternation, it has nevertheless met with
resistance from a substantial minority of church members, and there are still many parishes up and down the
country where Matins remains the principal Sunday
morning service. Enthusiasts for the Parish Communion
(who often include the incumbent of the recalcitrant
parish) usually argue along the following lines. The
Eucharist, they say, is the one really distinctive act of
regular Christian worship. By it, the congregation is
bound indissolubly together in a sacramental fellowship.
In the course of it, the worshippers make a symbolic
offering of themselves and all that their work has
produced. In return (though in no way earned by anything they have done) they receive the gift of God's
very self in the form of the sacrament. In short, it is the
service par excellence where 'something happens',
where the whole of Christian faith and experience is
gathered up and realized anew. It ought therefore to be
the principal service of the week.

The implication is, of course, that none of this is the
case at Matins, and therefore that those who insist on

preserving Matins as their main act of weekly worship are somehow missing the heart of the matter and persevering with a form of worship where (by comparison) 'nothing happens'; nothing is demanded of them (except the collection) and no sacramental grace is received. But to argue like this does less than justice to those many thousands of Anglicans (let alone the millions of Protestants in other churches) who in fact prefer to make a non-sacramental service their normal act of worship on a Sunday. It is also a gross over-simplification to say that nothing 'happens' at Matins or Evensong comparable with the sacramental action of the Eucharist. The point is important, and is worth further consideration for its own sake; but it also provides an excellent example of the way in which ordinary church members contribute to the belief of the church by their influence on public worship.

Ever since Cranmer's First Prayer Book of 1549, every authorized Prayer Book of the Church of England has begun with two services called 'Morning Prayer' and 'Evening Prayer'. These services were virtually Cranmer's creation. By immensely simplifying the medieval monastic offices (reducing the traditional seven 'hours of prayer' to two, and removing all the hymns, antiphons, responds and seasonal variations which had been added over the centuries), and by insisting on regular and systematic Scripture reading and recitation of the psalms, he provided the clergy and laity with a form of worship which was in due course to become the standard form of Sunday service in parish churches and cathedrals alike, and which is still greatly appreciated to this day. But it is fair to say that the success of Matins and Evensong has been something of an accident. These services have not been used as Cranmer intended them; yet for centuries they have been found to offer a satisfactory form for the regular worship of Anglican

33

congregations. The instinctive religious needs and attitudes of ordinary church members have in the long run prevailed over Cranmer's dogmatic directions and built around his services a pattern of worship he would hardly have recognized as his own creation.

An important part of Cranmer's original intentions can be read off the title which these services bear in the Book of Common Prayer: 'The Order for Morning (or Evening) Prayer *daily throughout the year*'. Cranmer was not thinking primarily of congregational worship on Sundays: he was starting from the daily devotions of monks and clergy, and by radically simplifying them, as well as translating them into English, he made them into acts of worship in which lay people could be expected to join. But there was another principle also in Cranmer's mind, which was of great importance to all the Reformers. In the words of one of the rubrics which are printed before Morning Prayer, the minister is commanded to say the daily service publicly, 'that the people may come *to hear God's word*, and to pray with him'. The primary purpose was not so much that people should join in a regular act of praise and devotion as that (in the words of Cranmer's own Preface of 1549) 'by daily hearing of Holy Scripture read in the church, they should continually profit more and more in the knowledge of God'. Cranmer conceived these services as above all a means by which every member of the Church would become familiar with the Bible. An important part of his Prayer Book was the lectionary, which provided for virtually the whole of the Old Testament to be read once each year and the New Testament three times; and there is great insistence in the rubrics on Scripture being read audibly and intelligibly, and upon the church being furnished and arranged to this end. There can be no doubt of the dominant image in Cranmer's mind when he conceived Morning

34

and Evening Prayer. It was of the minister reading a regular course of Scripture to his people, 'distinctly with a loud voice . . . standing and turning him so as he may best be heard of all such as be present'.

For centuries the Church of England has taken these services into its system and to its heart. But it is doubtful whether it has ever fully accepted Cranmer's intention that they should be primarily a means of learning the contents of the Bible. Even Cranmer himself was unable to be fully consistent. His lectionary divided up the Bible into sections to be read on every day of the year, and the Psalms on every day of the month. Its purpose was to make sure that Scripture was read continuously day after day, without interruption from ecclesiastical festivals and seasons; only in this way would the people get to know it properly. But, even so, he had to make concessions. The great holy days of the Church's year seem to demand the reading of appropriate lessons, and Cranmer duly allowed for this, even though it interrupted regular progress through each book of the Bible. Admittedly he allowed for it somewhat half-heartedly. In Holy Week, for instance, he prescribed special lessons only from the Old Testament, with the bizarre result that on Good Friday, if the calendar happened to fall that way, the New Testament lesson could even be an account of the resurrection. But the fact that he made any concession at all shows that he was unable to press his principle to its logical conclusion. Worshippers in church simply would not accept that the reading of Scripture in church is *only* for 'edification'.

Up to a point, of course, Cranmer's principle is certainly correct. One has only to think of the lesson reader standing at the lectern and facing the pews, or (still more) the preacher in the pulpit directly addressing every member of the congregation, to realize that part at least of what is going on is the passive reception by the listeners of words which are being addressed to them. Penitence, prayers and praises, one might say, are directed by the congregation towards God; in the lessons and the preaching it is more as if God, through the reader or the preacher, is addressing a word to the congregation. But this is by no means the end of the matter. Let us return for a moment to the point which we saw was conceded by Cranmer: that special holy days require special readings. Why is this so? It clearly is not (at least on major festival days) to teach or remind the people what the church is celebrating. On Christmas morning, the nativity story is uppermost in everyone's mind long before it is actually read out as a lesson. It is rather that we *have* to have this reading *because* it is Christmas Day. It is a necessary part of our celebration. If we did not have it, we would have left something undone.

We can be helped to see why this is so if we recall a point that was made in the last chapter. One of the distinctive things about the Christian Scriptures is that so much of them consists of narrative, of stories. Now stories – true stories – are important to us in many ways. We do not tell them only in order to apprise others of something that has happened. A married couple may remind each other of an event which was important to both of them; and by telling the story again they may relive something of that experience and feel more closely bound together. A ceremony in honour of a distinguished public figure will include some recital of his achievements: it is not that the audience is unaware of these things, but rather that a careful telling of the story seems an appropriate and necessary part of the ceremony. At the centenary of a school or college a speaker will run through the institution's history. He will not assume that people have never heard it before;

but the commemoration would be incomplete if it were
not publicly rehearsed on the day. All this, and more, is
true of the reading of Scripture in church. The Bible
contains the story of God's gracious dealings with men.
We read it, certainly, to be reminded of that story and
to learn more of its details. But we read it also as a way
of acknowledging God's goodness towards us, of celebrating the events which procured our salvation, and of
binding ourselves together as the community which has
received and which lives by this divinely inspired story.
It is something which (of course) we have received from
God; but it is also something which, in our worship, we
offer back to him.

It is clear from Cranmer's directions that he had en-
visaged none of this. His conception of the reading of
Scripture in church was exclusively for instruction and
'edification'. But only a few years later, when Richard
Hooker was defending the Prayer Book forms of worship against Puritan criticisms, he described the reading
of Scripture as 'a special portion of the service which we
do to God' – that is, not directed towards passive listeners as if *from* God, but offered as a constituent part of
worship *to* God. Hooker was making a theological point.
But, consciously or unconsciously, the style of worship
of the Church of England has again and again confirmed
his view. To take only one example: the lessons at
Matins and Evensong are very often read by a layman
who comes up to the lectern out of the congregation.
The reason for this is not (or not usually) that he or she
can be relied on to read the lesson more audibly and
intelligibly than the clergyman (though this may of
course happen to be the case). It is rather that it is felt
to be somehow appropriate for a member of the congregation – perhaps one who is in some way representative of the rest – to take responsibility for this part of
the service. The reading of the lessons is sensed not to

be a purely formal act (like the reading of minutes at a meeting) nor an act of straightforward instruction (like the reading of a lecture). It is part of a total act of worship; and those who undertake it are doing it 'for God' on behalf of the whole congregation. Indeed the more one compares the reading of Scripture in church with any other form of public reading or recitation, the more one sees the differences. How, for example, should one respond? If the lesson were really a piece of instruction, one would presumably take notes, ot at least try to keep it secure in the memory; if it were an academic lecture, one would applaud or ask questions. But the response required to a passage of Scripture read at a church service is quite different. That provided in the Book of Common Prayer follows a very old tradition: at the conclusion of each lesson we say or sing a canticle, that is, one of the oldest hymns of the Church. The prescribed response is an act of praise. Recently, our service books have been suggesting another: a short period of silence, which is equally an acknowledgement that the reading is to be responded to in a serious and personal way – we take its message into ourselves and then reply with praise and thanksgiving. Anglicans are not alone in this. Every denomination attaches some ceremonial, however slight, to the reading of Scripture in church. Visitors to Taizé, the community of Protestant origins in France, will have been struck by the degree of serious attention given to the lessons and expressed in a simple ceremonial; and it is well known that in the Orthodox Liturgy the ritual which precedes the reading of the gospel is comparable with that which accompanies the eucharistic offertory.

Even at this point, then, it is clear that the contrast from which we began, between a 'bare' service of Scripture and preaching on the one hand, and a full 'sacramental' service on the other, is much exaggerated.

There is a great deal which can be said to 'happen' at Matins and Evensong, whether simply said in a parish church or splendidly sung in a cathedral, and those who stubbornly prefer this form of worship in the face of all contemporary trends are not being merely conservative. They are preserving a tradition which has stood the test of time precisely because it contains and expresses many of those elements which are essential to any act of Christian worship. But, for our purpose, the important point is that the way these elements are preserved depends, not on the service book itself or the experts who devised it, but upon the parishes up and down the country which instinctively or deliberately order their worship in a certain way, and so contribute to the belief of the church about the nature of Scripture, of worship, and indeed of God himself.

We still have not touched on that element in public worship for which people have most affection and which influences their belief perhaps more powerfully than anything else – the hymns. Hymn-singing is un-doubtedly the most popular and unifying of all the activities that take place in church; and any standard hymn book contains (at least by implication) far more doctrine than the Book of Common Prayer. There is a sense, therefore, that what members of the Church of England believe can be read off from the hymns they love to sing. But, here again, it is a good deal more complicated than that. People sing and enjoy hymns for many different reasons. Unsatisfactory words can be redeemed and made popular by a good tune. Dated sentiments are acceptable because of their associations with traditional occasions. 'We plough the fields and scatter' is sung with enthusiasm despite its irrelevance to the occupations of the congregation and the methods of modern farming – a Harvest Festival would not be complete without it. That is to say: we must beware of

taking hymns more seriously than congregations themselves take them as indicators of belief. Not everyone
reflects on every word of a familiar hymn; and many
will sing a hymn with enjoyment and satisfaction because
of its tune or its associations, and happily disregard the
inappropriateness of some of its sentiments. But at the
same time there can be no denying the influence that
hymns exert upon each one of us. For one thing, they
are easily memorable – a factor which may become
even more significant in a period when new translations
of Scripture are increasingly often read in church. The
present generation of churchgoers may find that, if they
hear only modern versions of the Bible, they cannot
recall the words of a single one of the Beatitudes. But

> Blest are the pure in heart
> For they shall see our God

will stay in the mind permanently once it has been sung
a few times. For another, hymns occasionally have an
ability to convey Christian truth and Christian attitudes
of mind with great directness and immediacy:

> My richest gain I count but loss
> And pour contempt on all my pride.

People will be moved by these words who have never
warmed to the verses in Philippians on which they are
based. And an important feature of the hymn repertoire
of even the most modest congregations is its sheer
range – hymns from the early Middle Ages to the present day, hymns of every major denomination, hymns
for every Christian season, hymns for every personal
mood and public occasion. Some part of this great
treasury enters the religious consciousness of every
member of the church. Without it, our faith and worship – indeed, our belief – would be immeasurably
poorer.

But how, it may be asked, does the individual church member come into this? The hymns we sing are the hymns in our hymnbooks; they are chosen by the vicar or organist, who are often as much concerned with the tune and its familiarity as with the religious content of the words. Moreover the hymnbooks themselves are in no sense 'popular' collections. Those in most common use in England were compiled by highly specialized clergy and musicians, who sometimes had strong views of their own. The ordinary member of the congregation may seem to have little say in the choice of words which, through verse and music, are liable to become imprinted on his mind and subtly influence his beliefs. But in fact his say is decisive. The hymns which are sung in any church are the hymns which the congregation is happy, or at least willing, to sing. Hymns stand the test of time and find their way into hymnals because of their inherent strength and quality and because they express what the ordinary worshipper feels and believes. When they cease to do so, they are dropped and replaced. The ultimate arbiter is not the priest or the expert. It is the men and women in the pew who, by their enthusiasm or their disapproval, give a verdict on each hymn. In the long run their verdict is decisive.

Many hymns seem almost timeless. They have been sung for literally hundreds of years. But others have a shorter life. The sentimentality of many Victorian hymns now seems unacceptable: twentieth-century Christianity demands, and has been provided with, something more robust. New hymns are being composed in abundance: at least three new hymnals have found their way into parish churches in the last fifteen years. And these hymns also show a new emphasis, less on penitence and personal devotion, more on celebration and commitment. Whether these hymns reflect or generate the beliefs and attitudes of contemporary

41

church members is an unanswerable question: they probably do both. The important thing is that they were written in response to the needs of congregations, and, when they are used, it is a congregation which determines whether they are acceptable. Once accepted, they may indeed influence the beliefs of a whole generation of worshippers; but it was the worshippers themselves who first judged them to be consonant with their beliefs and gave them a place in their worship.

There are other elements in the worshipping life of the Church of England which are not written into any authorized Prayer Book but which have considerable significance as indicators of belief. The continuing popularity of the Three Hours Devotion on Good Friday (despite the lack of encouragement given to it by theologians and liturgical experts) shows, at the very least, that lay members of the church give the saving significance of the Cross a central place in their belief; and this centrality, in turn, is reinforced each time they attend the observance. Midnight services of Christmas, New Year and Easter are becoming increasingly popular, and suggest a growing need to impart a sense of drama – and of the out-of-the-ordinary – to the great festivals of the year. And the list could be extended. These are all manifestations of the same phenomenon: the expression and transmission of the needs and beliefs of ordinary members of the church through acts of worship which are not prescribed by ecclesiastical authority, and which run parallel, so to speak, with the set forms of service provided in authorized service books.

But to all this there is one important proviso. What we have been describing occurs in many places – but not in all. The picture of a congregation making careful and conscientious decisions about its pattern of worship, ensuring that Scripture is read with proper reverence and expectancy, taking responsibility for the choice of hymns and giving liturgical expression to new Christian experiences and insights, is a somewhat ideal one. Not all congregations have this degree of vitality and responsibility. To say therefore that in worship, as in other ways, lay members of the church ultimately influence the beliefs of the Church of England is to assume that the local church is alive to its tasks and opportunities. In many places this may not be so. There are still many congregations whom it is hard to rouse from a kind of conservative passivity. But it remains true, at least potentially, that each member of the church bears a responsibility (in the sense we have been exploring) for the beliefs of all of us; and when this is realized it could be a factor that will help to stir even the most sluggish parish to new life.

4
Reaching Consensus

Should divorced persons be remarried in church? Is a homosexual relationship sinful? Can women be ordained to the priesthood? Is a policy of nuclear deterrence incompatible with Christian principles?

All these questions, and many more, have been vigorously and earnestly debated in the Church of England in recent years. On all of them there have been discussions, reports and debates in General Synod. For the most part they appear to be theological questions, that is, ones that should be settled by reference to Christian principles rather than mere common sense; and certainly professional theologians as well as other prominent churchpeople have been involved in their discussion. Yet in most cases no agreed solution appears to have been found. The questions rumble on, the discussion fails to result in decision, the suffering caused by inadequate or indecisive church policy continues. At times it seems even as if the church is in danger of losing its credibility through its inability to make up its mind. What then has gone wrong? Or rather (perhaps we should ask), is this a sign of disease or of health? Would the church be a better place if things were otherwise?

It may be helpful to begin by describing the way in which the Church of England (like most other churches) sets about the task of finding and expressing its mind on such questions. It first sets up a commission or working party to examine the issue in detail. This is unlikely to include only theologians. Some there will certainly be; but there will also be experts in any technical field which is relevant (doctors, for instance, or psychologists in the case of homosexuality); there will be parish

44

priests; and there will be laymen (and now, increasingly, laywomen) whose main function is to make the group representative of the church at large. In due course this commission or working party will produce a report, which will be debated in General Synod. Its recommendations (if any) may be accepted in principle, or they may be rejected. If accepted, they will be 'commended for study' to diocesan and deanery synods, and after a period of wide discussion at different levels in the church specific proposals may be brought before General Synod which, if approved, may be held to express the mind of the church and will govern its conduct. Even then, there may still be many church members who dissent from these decisions, and who may succeed in having the discussion reopened at a later stage (as has happened in the case of the rules on divorced persons). But of course the report may have been rejected when it first came before Synod. In which case it will seem that the church has not yet been able to express its mind on the issue.

At first sight, the most puzzling feature of this whole procedure is the relatively small influence exerted by the theologians. Each report will usually start with an examination of the evidence from Bible and tradition; but it is very unusual for these strictly theological considerations to settle the issue, and the final recommendations may rest on many arguments other than strictly theological ones. That is to say, it will be clear from the report itself that those members of the commission (usually the majority) who are *not* theologians have played at least as decisive a part in the outcome. And the same is true of the subsequent discussions in General Synod and elsewhere. Theologians will continue to make an occasional, and sometimes influential, contribution. But the great majority of the speeches, and of the votes, will be given by church members with no particular theological competence, and it is by no means to be expected that they will docilely follow any clear lead which is given by the theologians.

In what sense, then, were we able to say at the outset that these questions are 'theological'? Our assumption was that they are matters on which the Christian religion has something to say. The logical way to proceed would seem to be to search the documents of the Christian tradition – Scripture, creeds, Articles of Religion; to identify those texts which are relevant to the point at issue; and to reach a firm conclusion in the light of them. And this is in fact how a church commission normally begins its work. The opening chapters of the report usually consist of a presentation and assessment of the theological evidence; certain key passages in Scripture are identified and discussed; a historical survey is given of the way in which the matter has been handled in the history of the Church; some tentative conclusions may be advanced. But this is by no means the end of the matter. The other members of the commission are there for a purpose. Some have a particular expertise to offer; all will have their say. The recommendations at the end of the report may seem at best loosely attached to the theological considerations at the beginning; and (as we have seen) they may be endorsed or rejected by assemblies many of whose members may have no theological competence at all.

This apparent failure of theology to carry the day is denied by some, lamented by others. Those who deny it will claim that far more theology enters the discussion at every level than I have allowed for; that the message of Scripture is clear; and that it is only the faithlessness of the church, its unwillingness to meet the challenge of the gospel, which prevents a clear answer from being given. On occasion this may be true. It can be said, for example, that the whole Bible shows a clear 'bias to the poor'; and it is hard to deny that the Church has throughout its history flourished more among the relatively rich than among the very poor, and that this indicates an unwillingness among its members to face some of the practical implications of the gospel. But in many other cases this can hardly be the explanation. The message of Scripture turns out not to be clear; debate necessarily involves consideration of factors other than strictly theological ones; and those who lament that there was 'not enough theology', either in the report itself or in subsequent debates, have to recognize that more theology does not necessarily result in clearer conclusions.

In part this is due to the simple fact that the world of today in which these questions have to be resolved is very different from the world in which the Bible, or indeed all the classical works of Christian theology, were written. A society in which one out of every four marriages ends in divorce, in which homosexual relationships are increasingly recognized and accepted, in which women exercise leadership and responsibility on the same terms as men, and whose existence is constantly threatened by nuclear confrontation, is a society so unlike that in which our spiritual forebears lived that we cannot expect the bare texts of Scripture, or the prescriptions of theologians who lived centuries ago, to give us clear guidance on the new and complex issues which face us today. Of course it can be said that certain things do not change. Human nature remains the same; and in the matter, say, of sexual morals there is no reason why the traditional teaching of the Church should not continue to provide a standard. For this reason many Christians believe that traditional church teaching on marriage and divorce, on sexual relationships within and outside marriage, on homosexuality

47

and on the position of women should be adhered to without further discussion. But one consequence of adopting this view would be that the church would rapidly dwindle into a small sectarian body: the majority of its present-day members are convinced that human nature is profoundly affected by its social environment, and would be quite unable to bind their children to a literal application of traditional teaching. And in any case most of the questions which are discussed today are genuinely new ones to which there is clearly no direct answer in Scripture or tradition. It follows that one of the first tasks of any commission or working party will be to understand the question as thoroughly as possible and determine just how new it is, just what issues it raises. Hence the contribution of experts other than theologians; hence the weight given to the experience of lay Christians who have encountered these problems in their personal or professional lives.

But the main reason why these questions seem so seldom to be settled by strictly theological reasoning lies in the nature of theology itself. We have already considered one reason why the Bible (which is the ultimate authority in Christian theological thinking) is ill adapted to provide the basis for systematic theological judgements: this is its narrative character, the fact that for the most part it is not offering doctrine or moral guidance but telling a story; and there is no direct route from a story to a formulation of belief or moral standards. But there is another reason: given that no part of the Bible speaks directly to the question in hand, there is a choice of passages which may be held to have a bearing upon it, and scholars and interpreters may legitimately disagree over which texts are more pertinent, which carry more weight, and which may be disregarded.

Take as an example the continuing debate over the

48

correct Christian attitude towards homosexual relationships. At first sight it may look as if an appeal to Scripture
will settle the matter once and for all. In the first chapter
of Romans St Paul refers to homosexual practices as
examples of conduct condemned by God and inevitably
drawing down punishment upon the perpetrators. But
closer study (as well as a natural repugnance for such a
sweeping and uncompassionate judgement) suggests that
we must use this passage with caution. St Paul was
referring specifically to the pagan world of his own
time, and judging it in the light of traditional Jewish
standards (which placed great store by family life and
abhorred all other sexual relationships). The problem of
homosexuals within the Christian community seems not
to have surfaced in his lifetime, and at most we have to
infer what he *would* have said about it had he been confronted with it. If we try to do this, we shall have to
look at a wider range of texts. We shall need to ask why
he wrote that 'it is better to marry than to burn', and
whether this has a bearing on the life together of homosexual couples; and we ought to consider also the
implications of his important criterion of moral conduct: 'does it build up the church?' If the condemnation
of homosexual relationships between persons who are
(or wish to be) devout and committed members of the
church results in harm to the whole body, then other
principles stated by St Paul must come into play: we
must bear the burdens of our weaker brother (Rom.
15.1); and in Christ there is no barrier between persons
of different race, status or sex (Gal. 3.28).

Now there is no calculus by which these different
considerations, all of which are based on Scripture, may
be weighed against each other. For some, the fact that
one passage seems to contain a clear and explicit judgement may seem all-important, despite the immense
differences between Paul's moral and cultural climate

and ours. For others, the principles of brotherly love, toleration and compassion (all based on Scripture) may outweigh any narrower considerations derived from a particular (and historically conditioned) text. Moreover, these two approaches, which seem to lead in this instance to incompatible conclusions, are by no means confined to this particular question. The first goes along with a general acceptance of the literal and literally applied meaning of Scripture, and for those who hold it to yield on this point would amount to a betrayal of a cherished principle: the enduring validity of Scripture taken in its literal sense. The second goes with a deliberate search for Christian priorities. There are times (many will feel) when mercy is more appropriate than judgement, love more important than discipline, tolerance a greater good than culturally conditioned conventions. To follow any individual text to a conclusion which is at variance with these great principles would amount to a betrayal of those priorities which are the result of attending to the message of Scripture taken as a whole. A difference of opinion over the bearing of Scripture on a particular moral issue is likely to reflect a difference of approach to the authority of Scripture altogether.

But theology is more than the Bible. A Christian study of a moral issue must also attend to what is called 'the Christian tradition'. This phrase requires some elucidation. There is no single Christian tradition, there are several; and it is necessary to declare which of them one is referring to. On many moral questions (such as the remarriage of divorced persons) the Eastern Orthodox churches have a practice different from that of the West; and to support it they appeal to their own very ancient tradition. This tradition is now becoming better known in the West, and reference is sometimes made to it in discussion of these questions. But the 'tradition' which is normally appealed to in Anglican theology is

50

'Western', that is to say, the teaching of the Roman Catholic Church, expressed in official documents or in the work of great theologians such as Thomas Aquinas, up to the time of the Reformation. Not that it necessarily stops there. Respectful attention is often given to more recent Catholic teaching, on the grounds that it represents a legitimate development of the earlier tradition. But at the same time the Protestant churches have each developed their own 'tradition' on certain matters. Where these are different from each other, or from the Roman Catholic tradition, they may carry weight only within their own denomination – the traditional Lutheran attitude to the complete autonomy of the state is a notable example: few would accept this 'tradition' who were not Lutherans themselves. In the case of the Church of England, the tradition (as we are coming to see in the course of this book) is more difficult to identify. It consists rather of a way of approaching moral questions than of particular solutions to them. Therefore when Anglicans refer to 'the Christian tradition' they usually mean that which has been taught in the church of the West up to the time of the Reformation, understood in the light of subsequent developments of that tradition in the contemporary Roman Catholic Church.

This brief elucidation of the concept of 'tradition' already indicates a reason why an appeal to tradition is not likely to settle the kind of issues with which we are concerned in this chapter. If there is more than one tradition, then a decision has to be made which, if any, tradition to follow; in the matter of the remarriage of divorced persons, for example, there is a number of different practices in the historic churches, each supported by their own 'tradition'; and there are now many in the Church of England who believe that our own exceptionally rigorous tradition might be modified in the direction of traditional Orthodox practice. But clearly, if we are going to have to *choose* between traditions, 'tradition' itself is not going to help us to make that choice. We shall have to bring in other considerations besides.

There is another reason why an appeal to tradition is unlikely to settle the matter. This is that new factors may have appeared which make the question quite different from what it was when the tradition was formulated. Take as an example the issue of the ordination of women. This is one matter on which the traditions of all the main churches were agreed until quite recent times; and this fact alone has considerable weight in the thinking of those who believe that any change in the Church's traditional practice of ordaining only men to the priesthood would be theologically unjustified. But now a number of provinces in the Anglican Communion, as well as most other Protestant churches, have introduced the change; and the reason given is that women have now assumed positions of responsibility in virtually every area of social life, in a way that would have been inconceivable when the Christian tradition was formed; that this represents a totally new factor in the situation; and that no appeal to traditional teaching, which was formulated without knowledge of this factor, can be decisive in settling the issue today.

A similar development has taken place over the question of homosexual relationships. It was argued in the Report, *Homosexual Relationships* (1979), that an entirely new factor has entered the discussion, namely the recognition that there is 'an area of human personality which has been identified only in comparatively recent times and which seems to have been largely unknown to the biblical writers. They appear to have had no conception of the "true" homosexual or the exclusively orientated homosexual condition as such' (p. 35). In the Bible, and for many centuries in the Christian tradition, it was taken for granted that homosexual relationships and practices were something indulged in deliberately and perversely by persons who were able to enter into 'normal' heterosexual relationships. The working party, with the authority given to it by those of its members who were distinguished representatives of the medical profession, declared that this assumption has now been shown to be false. There are people who *cannot* form a deep heterosexual relationship; a homosexual one is the only one open to them. It follows that neither the Bible nor the Christian tradition can offer a direct answer to their predicament (which was not recognized until quite recently). The church's response to the problem therefore involves a new assessment of biblical and traditional teaching in the light of new knowledge and new social circumstances. In this project, conflicting views may be legitimately held and expressed. In the event, the members of the working party confined themselves to 'conclusions expressed in carefully qualified terms' (p. 66). Their Report was modestly styled 'A Contribution to Discussion', and was promptly disowned by its sponsoring body (the Board for Social Responsibility). The Church of England now seems as far from having a policy on the matter as ever.

It appears, then, that no appeal either to Scripture or to tradition is likely to settle the kind of issues with which we have been concerned in this chapter. This is not to say that theology has nothing to say about them. To identify principles in the Bible which may be relevant, and to study the ways in which the Church has sought to apply these principles down the centuries, is an essential preparation for forming a Christian judgement. But we cannot expect theology to decide the question unaided. A working party which devoted an extra year to strictly theological study, or which

demanded that its membership should be stiffened by
the addition of more theologians, would not necessarily
come up with a more definite or persuasive answer. The
findings of theology still have to be tested against reason, common sense and experience of the modern
world; a choice still has to be made between one tradition and another of Christian thought; new social factors, new advances in knowledge, have to be taken into
account. And this involves enlisting the wisdom and
practical experience of others besides professional theologians – philosophers, experts, and ordinary lay men
and women.

We have seen that the price which has to be paid for
all this is the risk of failing to reach a decision. On
every single one of the questions mentioned at the
beginning (all of which are urgent and important) the
Church of England has not yet succeeded in forming a
clear opinion. We must return to our original question.
Is this failure to speak out on moral and religious issues
a sign of sickness and disorder in the church? Do we lose
all credibility by our apparent lack of moral conviction?
Or is a period of indecision a necessary stage in the
normal and healthy process of forming a corporate
Christian judgement?

One of the questions we have had in mind in this
chapter is that of the remarriage of divorced persons in
church. In 1971 an official Report was published on the
subject, which explicitly raised what the Commission
called 'The question of moral consensus'. The Commission had concluded, from a careful study of the evidence
in the Bible and tradition, that remarriage in church
(with due safeguards) '. . . would not be inconsistent
with the witness and teaching of the New Testament as
a whole; nor with the traditions of the Orthodox and
Protestant Churches; nor would it be inconsistent with
the Western Church . . . ' (*Marriage, Divorce and the*

54

Church, p. 72). It then went on to admit that 'these considerations are neutral'; they neither preclude nor support any change in the present practice of the Church of England. What arguments can then be used? The Commission proposed an appeal to a *moral consensus* of Christian people in the Church of England. It recalled that a similar appeal had been made to a moral consensus in 1958, when the Lambeth Conference for the first time sanctioned the use of contraception in family planning. 'In other words', wrote the Commission, 'at times the Church may have moral insight prior to and at least as fundamental as the theological insight needed to explain it'; and it went on to argue that if it were found that a moral consensus in fact obtains in the Church of England to support the remarriage of divorced persons, then it would be proper to make the change.

This notion of a consensus did not win immediate approval: indeed considerable hostility to it was expressed in the subsequent debate in General Synod. Surely, it was argued, a course of action is either right or wrong. To appeal to a consensus is in effect to lay the matter before the judgement of private individuals, who may have all sorts of reasons for deciding one way or the other, some personal, some due to prejudice, some arising out of sheer ignorance of Christian principles. Surely we must possess some more objective criterion than this? But these objections betrayed a misunderstanding of the proposal. The Commission was careful to specify that what they had in mind was not a general moral consensus throughout the country, but one 'among Christian people in the Church of England' – a consensus, in other words, based on Christian faith and practice. This gives us an important clue to the way in which moral decisions are in fact reached in the church.

Let us take as a final example the contemporary

debate on what is perhaps the most urgent question of all: the attitude of the church towards a policy of nuclear deterrence. Here, if anywhere, there is surely a question with profound moral implications; and here, surely, is an issue on which Christian principles can be brought to bear. Moreover, if the Church of England were to speak with a clear and unambiguous voice on it, this might have a significant influence upon the policy which the government of the time found it possible to pursue. Yet the church (in this country at least) has made no clear pronouncement. Christians seem confused, and far from unanimous. Does this mean that they are failing to witness to the truth? Is the church asleep or moribund? Is not the individual church member entitled to better guidance than this?

Perhaps the first thing to be said is that questions concerning war and the use of violence are and always have been notoriously difficult for Christians to agree upon. From the early centuries of its history the Church has included among its members those who hold virtually incompatible views on such matters. Some have found any kind of involvement in military service, or any willing co-operation with their country's preparations for the possibility of war, totally irreconcilable with the teaching of Jesus. Others have recognized the absolute duty of the state to provide for the security of its subjects, even to the point of going to war if the nation or its allies are seriously threatened, and feel obliged to serve the state when it is responsibly fulfilling this duty. So, down the centuries, there have been Christian pacifists and Christian non-pacifists, Christians who refuse to be involved in war under any circumstances and Christians who are willing to serve in the armed forces. The entry of nuclear weapons into the debate cannot necessarily be expected to resolve this age-old debate.

It is a debate in which an appeal to Scripture has not greatly advanced matters: both sides can find support in the Bible for their point of view, and there is no reason to think that any advances in our understanding of Scripture are going to make a significant difference. On the other hand, an important role has been played by tradition. Those who believe that a Christian may approve of war and even engage in it himself have never thought that this would hold of any war whatever. For a Christian, war is acceptable, if at all, only under certain conditions; and there is a long theological tradition which has sought to define (under the heading of 'The Just War') precisely what those conditions should be. Not that, as a matter of history, wars in which Christians have been involved have ever in fact conformed to these conditions; even the Crusades, which were presented to the faithful as a high Christian enterprise, turned out to be anything but a 'Just War'. Nevertheless there was certainly an intention in the minds of Christian rulers to adhere to these principles, even if in practice their wars turned into something quite different; and it is on this basis that countless Christians have taken part in warfare with a relatively clear conscience.

One of these principles is that any means used in war should be strictly in proportion to the end to be achieved: there is no moral justification for causing more damage, suffering and death than is strictly necessary to gain the object for which the war is being waged. It is at this point that nuclear weapons seem to have introduced a new factor into the argument. It is widely agreed that their use would always be disproportionate; the damage that would be caused to life and property is totally without relation to any possible gain which might follow from their use. In particular, the casualties which might be inflicted on civilian populations, both at the moment of detonation and subsequently through long-term illness and genetic malformation, represent a risk which is totally unacceptable to the Christian conscience. It would seem therefore that a war which involved the use, or even the threat, of nuclear weapons could never fulfil one of the basic conditions of the Just War; it could never be conducted with the kind of restraint which (according to this Christian tradition) alone makes it possible for a Christian to take part with a clear conscience. It follows that the introduction of nuclear weapons has presented Christians with a new situation. Those who previously felt able to take part in a war so long as (at least in intention) certain conditions were observed, must now (since those principles *cannot* be observed) dissociate themselves from war and become pacifists.

Many Christians in this country have in fact followed the logic of this argument and declared themselves totally opposed to any policy which involves the possession of nuclear weapons. And yet we find that this logic seems not to be sufficient to persuade a clear majority of their fellow-Christians to take the same view. The church continues to contain at least as many supporters of a policy of nuclear deterrence as it does unilateralists. It speaks, now as so often before, with a divided voice. Why is this so?

At this point it is necessary to ask a different kind of question altogether. Which is more important (and indeed more Christian): to come to the right conclusion about the morality of any future war waged with nuclear weapons; or to do all one can to prevent such a war ever happening? There is a very large number of people (not only Christians) who believe that the whole idea of nuclear warfare is utterly immoral – on this, at least, there is general agreement among Christians, and all the main churches have issued statements to this effect. But by no means all who subscribe to

58

this consensus go on to adopt a pacifist position, that is, to dissociate themselves personally from any policy of deterrence which involves the possession of nuclear weapons. Many see it as their clear Christian duty to do all in their power to reduce the risk of war and to promote general disarmament. The question they see as the most pressing one is that of the most effective way to achieve these aims. Some genuinely believe (having calculated the consequences so far as is possible) that a unilateral renunciation of nuclear weapons would make a significant contribution to world peace and security; others place their reliance upon those factors for which impressive historical arguments can be summoned in support: the preservation of a balance of power sufficient to deny any advantage to an attacker; sustained diplomatic and political activity to reduce tension and create stability; and the meeting of any military threat (including that of a nuclear arsenal) with an answering threat strong enough to deter aggression.

We can now see more clearly that those who hold these different views on the best way to prevent nuclear war ever taking place are not disagreeing on *Christian* principles at all. The difference between them is not a theological one or even a moral one: it is prudential. They disagree only on the purely practical question of how best the risk of nuclear war may be eliminated. Different opinions on this question are found among political leaders, senior officers in the armed forces, military strategists and scientists; there is no reason why different opinions should not also be held in the church (which, after all, includes many people who belong to these categories). It would be entirely inappropriate to expect *the church* to have a single and united view on a practical question over which expert and responsible people are deeply divided.

It is not therefore a sign of failure on the part of the

church if it does not make a clear judgement on the issue of (for example) unilateral versus multilateral disarmament. The question (for many of those who debate it) is a practical one, and the church has no special expertise to bring to it. On the other hand it would be equally wrong to assume that the church has nothing to say on the matter. Principles are involved which are profoundly moral, profoundly Christian; it is only their correct application which is in dispute. Perhaps we are now in a position to see what might count as sickness and what as health in the life of the church as it tries to face this crucial issue.

It would be a sign of sickness

(1) if a majority of the members of the Church of England allowed themselves to be persuaded that the Bible offers a direct and simple answer to the question. There exist extreme fundamentalist sects which find in certain texts in the Book of Revelation clear prophecies of an imminent world-wide cataclysm; they identify this with a nuclear war; and they draw the conclusion that such a war is inevitable and is according to the will of God. We have seen that the part played by Scripture in the Church of England is quite incompatible with such a naive approach.

(2) if the church came to a decision which made it impossible for both pacifists and non-pacifists to continue to belong. We have seen that this fundamental difference has existed in the church almost since the beginning, and that there are good reasons why the advent of nuclear weapons has not turned us all into pacifists. It could not be a proper expression of 'the mind of the church' if a substantial number of its members felt excluded by it.

(3) if the church ignored the experience and judgement

of those of its members (and they are many in the Church of England) who bear some responsibility in government and in the armed forces. We have seen that their assistance is essential if we are to understand correctly the problems upon which Christian principles have to be brought to bear; and a 'church view' which they found they were unable to go along with in their professional lives could not be regarded, in any representative sense, as the mind of the church. We have no business to unchurch some of our most responsible (and often most deeply reflective and committed) members.

(4) if, in view of all these difficulties, a majority of church members took the view that the church cannot have anything to say on the subject.

It would be a sign of health if Christians at all levels of the church were striving to relate their faith to the problem in all its complexity. This involves different kinds of expertise. There is that of the theologians, who help us to see what there is in Scripture and tradition which bears on the issue. There is that of politicians, servicemen and scientists, whose knowledge is essential for exploring the implications of any course which commends itself on Christian grounds. And besides this, there is the good sense and moral conscience of all those who seek to conform their lives and thinking to the example of Christ and who pray, worship and reflect in company with their more expert fellow-Christians. On many aspects of the problem, and in particular (as we have seen) in the field of political and strategic options, there is almost bound to be disagreement; but the best sign of health the church could exhibit would be an ability to reach a consensus on certain principles which must be observed in any event.

It is precisely such a consensus which seems to have

been emerging in recent years, not just in the Church of England, but among Western Christians generally. Partly this consists of agreement on general principles which are not often called into question – the immorality of indiscriminate attack on non-combatants, and the evil effects of weapons whose lethal power is out of all proportion to any gain that could be achieved. But there is also a growing recognition that we agree on a more specific point. As a bishop has recently expressed it in a letter to *The Times* (9th June 1983)

> There are no circumstances that would justify the *first use* of any nuclear warhead of whatever size or style.

This principle, which was agreed by the General Synod of the Church of England in November 1982, and affirmed in the Pastoral Letter of the Roman Catholic Bishops in the U.S.A. in 1983, is the result of just the kind of deliberative process we have been describing; it can be said to represent a 'moral consensus among Christian people in the church'; and it represents a fundamental criticism of the strategy to which the western nations are at present committed (NATO seeks at present to deter massive Russian aggression by conventional forces with the threat of nuclear retaliation – i.e. 'first use'). Such a clear conclusion, reached after attending both to Christian principles and to the realities of the present situation, and bearing so directly upon the choices open to politicians, is surely a sign of health in the church – if not of hope for the world.

5
Consolidating and Advancing

The impression given so far may well be that the Church of England makes up its doctrine as it goes along. Attention to Scripture, participation in worship, responsible concern for moral attitudes and decisions – this is what forms the 'mind' of the Church of England and creates the material out of which, from time to time, an Anglican theologian, or perhaps a Doctrine Commission, may attempt to formulate 'what the Church believes'.

But is this so? What about the Thirty-nine Articles? Are not these an authoritative statement of the Church's doctrine, which every parish priest in the Church of England is supposed to read aloud at his first public service in his church, and to which every clergyman has to give his assent? His Majesty's Declaration, prefixed to the Articles in the Book of Common Prayer in 1628 and still printed with them, states that 'they do contain the true Doctrine of the Church of England agreeable to God's Word'. Should they not therefore provide the solution to all our problems?

The simplest way to answer this question is to look up the Articles in any Prayer Book and see whether they tell us all we need to know about the doctrine of the church. We can see at a glance that they do not. The first eight articles, admittedly, address themselves to fundamental matters of the Christian faith: the Trinity, the incarnation, the holy Scriptures and the creeds. But the topics which follow – original sin, justification by faith, predestination – belong to the doctrinal debates of the Reformation; and the remaining articles are mainly devoted to practical questions which were of importance in the sixteenth century but have little import for most of us today. It could not possibly be said that the Articles tell us what the Church of England believes. Indeed, they were never intended to do so.

Nevertheless, the question was not a foolish one. The notion that a church might publish a statement of its belief, and require assent to that statement from its ministers, or even from all its members, is one that is familiar in a number of the churches which were born at the Reformation. Indeed these 'confessions', as they were called, formed the doctrinal basis of a number of continental churches, and the so-called Westminster Confession (1646) is still the foundation document of Presbyterian churches. As recently as the nineteen thirties, the 'Confessing Church' in Germany based its opposition to the Nazis on a Declaration of Christian principles which they believed must not be compromised through any arrangement with the State. Moreover, the influence of two of the continental Reformation 'Confessions' – those of Augsburg and Würtemberg – can be traced in the composition of our own Articles. From the point of view of history, there would be nothing surprising in a Protestant church beginning its life with an explicit statement of the doctrine it proclaims.

And yet, whatever may be the case in other churches, the Thirty-nine Articles of the Church of England have never had the status of a 'Confession of Faith'. For one thing, they are never appealed to on their own. In every formula of the 'assent' which clergymen have had to give them, they have always been coupled with the Book of Common Prayer and the Ordinal, and there has never been any suggestion that they should replace the creeds, still less the Scriptures. At most, they might be called 'the Church of England's confessional supplement to the Catholic creeds' (*Believing in the Church*, p. 115). Moreover there has been great uncertainty, ever since the Articles were published in 1571, about the extent to which the clergy (and to a lesser extent the laity) must be obliged to 'subscribe' to them. At the time, the Articles stated a position on a number of issues which were being vigorously debated by different parties in the church. They could be interpreted, in other words, as a threat; if you want to belong to the Church of England, this is the position you must hold. But did this mean that if you could not conscientiously accept, say, the judgement of Article XXI on the fallibility of all General Councils of the Church, you must cease to be a member of the Church of England? Are not some things more important than others? Must we subscribe to all the articles, rather than just those which touch the essentials of the faith? Or is there some way in which we can *interpret* certain articles so that they will seem more acceptable?

These questions continued to be discussed for a long time, and in the seventeenth century minor adjustments were made in the law concerning subscription. Throughout the eighteenth century and well into the nineteenth devout clergymen in the Church of England continued to feel qualms of conscience about a form of 'subscription' which seemed to imply their full assent to certain doctrinal matters which they no longer saw in the same way as their sixteenth-century predecessors. Things came to a head in the 1860s. By this time a substantial number of clergy, under the influence of the Oxford Movement, had moved towards a distinctly 'Catholic' approach to matters on which the Articles seemed to them stridently 'Protestant'. The result was that clergy became required, not to 'subscribe', but to 'assent' (a more non-committal expression), and to declare the truth, not of the Articles as such, but of 'the Doctrine of the Church of England, as therein set forth'. This provided some relief, but the problem was not solved. It was increasingly felt that (for example) the statements on Original Sin and Predestination in the Articles use language and concepts (mainly derived from St Augustine) which are no longer those in which we express our faith today. The Articles, in fact, were in the eyes of many far too 'dated' to provide an expression of contemporary belief; and so, in 1975, a Declaration of Assent passed into law which bound the clergy of the Church of England to nothing more threatening than 'belief in the faith . . . to which the historic formularies of the Church of England bear witness'.

On thing is clear from this fragment of history. The Articles have never been an answer to the question, 'What does the church believe?' At most, in the sixteenth century, they stated the position of the Church of England on certain disputed matters in such a way that the majority of clergy could conscientiously subscribe to them. Today, their language and their presuppositions seem to belong to such a remote age that few members of the Church of England would recognize their own faith in them at all. In the 1975 Declaration of Assent they are just one of the 'historic formularies' of the Church of England. To understand them, we have to know our Reformation History. To apply them today, we have presumably to argue something like this: if, in the sixteenth century, the Church of England adopted that position on that issue, what position should it adopt in the twentieth century on an issue which may be quite different? If the application is as difficult as this, it is not surprising if few people ever refer to them for an answer to a question of doctrine.

Yet there is one aspect of this history which points to a less negative conclusion. We have seen that other churches of the Reformation produced a 'Confession' rather similar to our Articles, and that certain continental Confessions actually provided models for their compilation. These Confessions were necessary as a means by which a new Protestant church could identify itself over against the Roman Catholic Church and against other new churches: it needed to state clearly what it believed that was different from what others believed; and it was this common belief which enabled its members to know that they belonged to the same church. The situation in England was both similar and different. There were things to be said in opposition to the Roman Catholic Church; hence the attacks on 'Romish Doctrine' in the Articles. But, unlike the Protestant churches abroad, the Church of England claimed to be 'Catholic' as well as 'Reformed'. Its continuity with the past was as important as its reforms in the present. A great deal of its doctrine, therefore, could be taken as read; what its members believed was what Christians in the catholic church of the West had always believed. Its identity did not depend (as with the continental churches) on a total position over against Rome; only on certain matters must there be a repudiation of 'Romish Doctrine'. Moreover, whereas each continental church rapidly acquired its distinctive character and so separated itself from the others, the object of the Elizabethan Settlement was the exact opposite: to create a Church of England which would include all the Christians in the country. This was, of course, an impossible ideal. There has never been a time when all English Christians have happily belonged to the Established Church. But the vision was there from the start, and profoundly affected even the writing of a 'confessional' document like the Articles. The object was not to exclude those who did not agree, but to formulate the doctrinal identity of the Church of England in such a way that the great majority of the English people could feel they belonged. The object was not to exclude but to include. It is in this respect that the Articles can still help us to respond as Anglicans, in the tradition of the Church of England, to the challenge of a world which often demands that we say what it is that we believe. Our whole tradition (of which the Articles are an important part) warns us against doing so in a way which will unchurch those who cannot quite accept the way we say it, but nevertheless feel a deep allegiance to the Church of England.

The Articles are not the only attempt in the history of the Church of England to state at least part of the church's doctrine. In 1922 the Archbishops set up a Commission which in 1938 issued its Report entitled *Doctrine in the Church of England.* This, unlike the Articles, covered all the main areas of Christian belief; but being a book of some two hundred pages its purpose was also different. No one could be expected to 'assent' to it in the sense of swallowing it in a single mouthful. The hope was rather that individuals in the church would find their beliefs more or less expressed in it, and recognize it as a kind of standard against which their own orthodoxy could be measured. The background to the Commission's work was the sense which prevailed between the two World Wars that the Church of England was attempting to embrace an impossibly wide range of opinions. Could clergymen who seemed to hold virtually opposite views on a number of important matters (such as the question of what happens at the Eucharist, the propriety of offering prayers for the dead, or the degree to which Scripture may be allowed to be in error) continue to be loyal ministers in one and the same church? In the words of the Commission's terms of reference, its brief was 'to consider the nature and grounds of Christian doctrine with a view to demonstrating the extent of existing agreement within the Church of England and with a view to investigating how far it is possible to remove or diminish existing differences'. In this task, the Commission was reasonably successful. Its report became a standard point of reference by which believers, clergy and theologians of different persuasions could tell how far they were really Anglicans, and what opinions would run the risk of being identified as incompatible with the faith and practice of the Church of England. Along with the Prayer Book and the Articles, it became one of the sources from which it is possible to distil an answer to the question, What does it mean to be a member of the Church of England?

Yet the book is seldom referred to. For nearly twenty years it was out of print. Is it already so dated? Or is it rather that the questions being asked now are different from those that were being asked fifty years ago? Then, as we have seen, the problem was to reconcile different shades of belief in the Church. Now, it is to find means of expressing the Christian faith in a way that makes sense to our contemporaries. Then, the main threat to the church seemed to be its divisions. Today, its whole credibility is at stake. Small wonder that a statement of doctrine written for one set of circumstances should have little to say in another. Or to put it another way: doctrine is never declared in a vacuum. In the sixteenth century the Articles were compiled to mark a boundary over against the Roman Catholic Church on the one hand and certain extreme forms of Protestantism on the other. In the nineteen twenties and thirties the need was to find common ground between different tendencies in the Church of England itself. Today, the problem is to make Christianity credible to those brought up in a secular world view and a pluralist society. Clearly the work of formulating doctrine has to be done anew. But one principle at least remains constant. Each time a doctrine is declared there is a risk of excluding from the church someone who cannot accept it. In the case of the Thirty-nine Articles, this risk was taken deliberately: it might be necessary to exclude covert Roman Catholics or extreme Protestants. In 1938 the risk was minimized. 'No one would be silenced or made liable to heresy hunts', declared the Preface; but at the same time it would be possible to identify teaching that was 'opposed and contradictory to this statement of doctrine', with the implication that those who taught it could at least be prevented from doing so in the name of the church. There is now a demand for a declaration of doctrine in the nineteen eighties. How will this principle be applied? Will anyone have to be unchurched?

The question was raised in a sharp form by the publication of *Honest to God* in 1963, and again by that of *The Myth of God Incarnate* in 1977. These books caused widespread shock and scandal. Was it really possible, it was asked, for a bishop of the Church of England to use such apparently irreverent language about God and to suggest one could say one's prayers while cleaning one's teeth? Was it really in order for a Regius Professor of Divinity to suggest that the incarnation was a 'myth'? Surely these books were a damaging attack on the Church's faith, made worse by being launched by distinguished members of the church itself? Surely the church ought to have made an authoritative reply in defence of its traditional doctrine? Then at least we would have known where we stood!

In fact a reply was made: to *Honest to God* by the Archbishop of Canterbury in a pamphlet (Michael Ramsey, *Image Old and New*, 1963); to *The Myth of God Incarnate* by a group of mainly evangelical clergymen (Michael Green, ed., *The Truth of God Incarnate*, 1977). But in neither case was this regarded as an authoritative response by the church, nor would the authors have expected their work to be received in this way. It was rather that the publication of each of these two apparently radical books set off a debate in the church of which we are still feeling the effects. Let us see, in rather more personal terms, how this works out in practice.

A scholar-bishop lies in bed in hospital. During three months of enforced leisure he looks again at some of the more radical theology that has been appearing since the war – Bultmann, Bonhoeffer, Tillich – and reviews his own understanding of the faith in the light of it. Christian people, he believes, along with many other searchers after faith, are finding it increasingly difficult (as he is) to reconcile the traditional language and images by which God is described and worshipped with the realities of present day experience, the scientific understanding of the universe, and the insights into our own human nature provided by modern psychology. But does this mean that we can no longer believe in God? Surely not. The task is rather to find a new language, new concepts, in which to express our faith. God is the 'Ground of our Being'. Christ is 'a man for others'. Holiness and prayer mean taking the circumstances of our daily lives, not less, but more seriously. We must take the risk of giving up our old images of a God 'out there', of Jesus as a supernatural saviour, of our faith as the practice of a 'religion'. We must take this world seriously; only then shall we find the God who is the ultimate ground of the world and of ourselves; only then shall we be 'Honest to God'.

At the time this seemed heady stuff (though none of it was, or should have been, new to theologians). To countless puzzled people it seemed a liberation. Many of them had harboured similar thoughts themselves; many more were conscious of the constraints placed upon their religious thinking and practice by the traditional language of the Church and its ministers. And here was a bishop, no less, not afraid to voice some of their own deep dissatisfaction and apparently authorizing a new

71

freedom of language about God and Christ and a new style – more relaxed, informal and 'secular' – of Christian living. But others were outraged. To call God the 'Ground of our Being' was to abandon all belief in a transcendent God. To call Christ simply 'a man for others' was to deny his divinity. To say that 'Nothing is prescribed – except Love' was to open the door to a drastic relaxation of Christian moral standards. So the cry went up: why doesn't the church do something? Someone ought to say where we stand!

Bishop Robinson's opponents got something of what they wanted when the Archbishop of Canterbury gave him a public but half-hearted warning not to allow his views to be mistaken for the teaching of the church. But what followed was not a heresy-hunt. What followed was what a subsequent book called *The Honest to God Debate*. And now, twenty years later, we can see that the debate has been good for us all.

This story is as good an example as one could wish of an essential aspect of 'Believing in the Church'. The Christian faith has never consisted simply of a series of doctrinal formulas handed down from generation to generation. The changing circumstances of each successive age have made it necessary to find new ways of expressing the old truths and new styles of Christian discipleship. Caution is of course necessary, and conservatism often seems the safest policy. It is essential that, however much the clothing may change, the body of the faith should be passed on intact. But at the same time, if no serious attempt is made to interpret the faith to those whose intellectual presuppositions and moral standards are totally different from those of early Christianity, there is a danger of the church losing touch with society and slowly withering away. Who, then, is responsible for this necessary process of continual reformulation? For the most part (as is becoming clearer as this book proceeds) it is the lay members of the church themselves. It is they who are in daily contact with the non-Christian world; it is they who have to find words in which to account for 'the hope that is in them'; it is they who constantly test the teaching they receive against the reality of their secular lives and the incomprehension of their neighbours, workmates and friends. But it is also the clergy and theologians; for it is primarily they who have the learning and the opportunity to reflect deeply on the problems and attitudes of contemporary society, and to bring the Christian faith to bear on them.

But, as in all fields of human enquiry and enterprise, this is not an even and constant process. Some periods see relatively little change; some require consolidation rather than advance; others are times of rapid change, challenge and radical questionings. Progress often comes in a quiet way through the gradual adoption of a new idiom or a new style. But (as in science, or art) the most profound changes are often the result of the appearance of a completely new idea, a flash of insight from a genius, or the steady pursuit of a radical concept to its logical conclusion. The church, like an army, needs its sappers and snipers, sometimes deep behind the enemy's lines; like an exploration party, it needs its adventurers and pioneers, way out in front; like a research team, it needs members capable of following a totally new line of thought that will ultimately modify the whole programme. In a word, the church needs its radical theologians.

But all depends on how their explorations are received. These are men and women who take considerable personal risks. Their line of thought will put their own faith under strain long before that of their readers or hearers. They are deliberately forgoing the protection and support of their colleagues and fellow-believers.

73

They well know what alarm and dismay their conclusions may cause. But (though they are often accused of the opposite) their quest is deadly serious. They are not deliberately making light of traditional Christian doctrines. They are resolutely facing the difficulties and strains which the world of today places upon their beliefs, and seeking ways in which they can continue to articulate their faith with integrity. A timid or moribund church is one that instantly disowns them if their explorations seem to lead into dangerous territory, or that waits to see whether ecclesiastical authority will censure or silence them. A healthy church is one that can receive the stimulus of such thinking, test its value in the light of Christian experience and daily living, and draw from it such help and inspiration as may ultimately lead to new understanding and growth. And this again is the responsibility, directly or indirectly, of every member of the church. It is only as new tactics, ideas and concepts are received into the real centre of church life, reflected upon, tested in practice, and combined with others in the light of traditional teaching and values, that doctrine will continue to be a living force in the lives of Christians and in the life of the church. The enduring consequence of *Honest to God* was not the notoriety of Bishop Robinson but the widespread participation of church members in 'The Honest to God Debate'. Today the area of debate has shifted. It is the nature and status of Christ, and the meaning of the concept of divine providence in a world apparently determined by a complex chain of natural causes, which our more adventurous theologians are calling into question. In the long run, the value of their contribution will depend, not on the stir it causes at the time or the sharpness of an official church 'response', but on the willingness of members of the church to accept the challenge it poses to their own beliefs and to test, in their praying, thinking and living within the community of the church, the viability of these new avenues of thought.

6

Boundary Maintenance

'That children might be brought up in the fear and nurture of the Lord . . . '

'That he may learn the Creed, the Lord's Prayer, and the Ten Commandments, and all other things which a Christian ought to know and believe to his soul's health.'

This is how, in the seventeenth century, the Book of Common Prayer set out the duty of parents and god-parents to pass on the faith to the next generation. The system was extremely simple and perfectly clear. Children would learn the rudiments of the faith from their parents. Those who went to school would find themselves in a Christian environment where further religious instruction would be given. Later, as a great network of Church of England schools and Sunday schools spread over the land, Christian parents were given a comforting assurance that, simply by receiving education, their children would become deeply imbued with the faith of the Church of England and be equipped, in their turn, to pass it on to their own children. And so an essential continuity was preserved.

In making this matter of Christian education a high priority, the church resembles a great number of other institutions and organizations. Controlling and passing on information is in fact one of the main functions of most of the 'systems' which surround us. Take the practice of medicine. This is carried on almost entirely on the basis of knowledge and skill which each practitioner has learnt from others. But it is vitally important for the effectiveness and standards of the medical profession that this process of learning should be *systematic*. It cannot be left to each aspiring doctor to pick up knowledge and skills in a random way from any source whatever – new books and old, British and Chinese medicine, herbal and homeopathic practitioners, faith healers and chiropractors. For medicine to be generally effective, and for medical science to progress, it has to be *organized*. Training and information must be given in recognized institutions according to agreed standards. Only if these conditions are observed will it be clear who counts as a doctor and who does not. The science and practice of medicine cannot continue without a carefully controlled system of education and training.

The same is true of all the sciences and all the professions. No one can contribute effectively to scientific research who has not been trained and educated in the generally accepted methods and data of the subject. None of us would trust ourselves to an airline pilot who had not been passed as competent by an authorized body, any more than we would entrust our affairs to a lawyer who had no professional qualification. It is true also of business and industry. Business cannot function unless every employee has a certain stock of knowledge and certain skills. All must know the aims and purpose of their activity (whether it is fitting a car door or building up a market for cars in a distant country). All must know the procedures for producing the desired result. All must know something of the organization of the concern, at least so far as it affects the individual employee. And it is an absolute priority for the business to make sure that everyone gets this necessary information from authorized sources – not from gossip and hearsay, out-of-date manuals, or political propaganda. A business must be *systematic* in its control and organization of information.

Here then is something which virtually all the institutions and organizations which surround us have in common: the systematic control of the information which is required for the institution to continue and flourish. Here, 'systematic' simply means that things are not left to chance. If the members of an organization were left entirely to their own devices, to pick up skills and information in any way they chose, the organization would not survive. The identity and continuance of any corporate human activity depend on some 'system' for the transmission of information. In recent years these 'systems' have come under intensive study in their own right. It has been observed that in many respects they all behave in the same way; and this observation can actually be useful, in so far as if an organization is in trouble it may be possible to diagnose its sickness as a failure to observe a basic principle of systematic information–transmission.

Can this so-called 'systems analysis' tell us anything about the Church of England? Before we try to answer this question we must clear away some possible objections. First, I have been talking as if the primary purpose of a system is to control and transmit *information*; but this is hardly an appropriate description of the characteristic activities of the church. Christians do not go to church primarily to obtain or convey information. Their main spiritual activity – worship and prayer – even if it is in some sense 'communication' with God, is hardly a matter of conveying 'information' to him about themselves or to themselves about God. Their main practical activity – service offered to fellow human beings – is again not mainly a matter of teaching or informing; it is better described by such words as 'giving', 'serving' and 'caring'. But we must beware of using the word 'information' too narrowly. It is true that words – verbal messages of one kind or another –

are a very important means of conveying information; but they are not the only means. A lover conveys his feelings by his eyes, his gestures, his smiles and silences as much as by the stammering sentences in which he tries to express them. A conductor has to convey his meaning entirely by signs; he has a number of words at his disposal (such as Toscanini's famous *cantando*), but these are available only in rehearsal; at the performance he must find means of communicating without them. And it is the same with a Christian. Sometimes he has to give a verbal account of 'the hope that is in him'; but more often he conveys his faith by the style of his life, by his care for others, his attention to prayer and his enjoyment of worship. 'Information' therefore is being used in this context in a wider sense. The Church has to be able to formulate and teach its faith in verbal doctrines; but this is not its only or even its primary task. It also transmits its faith through worship, through example, through acts of self-sacrifice and service. For the purpose of the argument, all these count as 'information'.

Secondly, we must try not to let the question become confused by some of our very natural feelings about 'systems' in general. For many of us, what we call 'the system' has become an object of intense distrust. It is precisely because they have grown into large impersonal systems that so many institutions which were intended to be to our advantage – such as medical practice, social services, the provision of public transport – have become threatening and apparently hostile. But the fact that some systems may be oppressive and sinister does not make systems themselves any less necessary for our well-being. Without some systematic framework, constructive human activity is virtually impossible. We cannot go through life leaving everything to chance. We cannot enjoy our freedom without knowing

79

the limits beyond which we cannot go. A minimum of *order* is essential for life. As we shall see, no individual need be totally controlled by the system; each of us lives in constant tension with some aspect of it, and this is what enables us to be creative members of it. But a system there must be if anything is to be achieved at all; and to say that the Church is a system is to say no more than that it shares certain features with every other form of social organization and institution.

After these preliminaries, let us return to our question whether we can learn anything from this approach about the Church of England. In some respects religions, and religious institutions, are particularly good examples of systematic behaviour. The information that they have to preserve and transmit is believed to be of the very greatest importance to individual members: it is their 'word of life', their assurance of salvation. Moreover it is sacrosanct. Political parties may change their constitution, universities their syllabuses, business enterprises their range of operations and methods. But a religion or a church is the guardian of something 'given'. The information it has to pass on to its adherents is divinely authorized; by definition it is the same as it was in earlier generations, however much it may need reinterpretation and reformulation to meet the needs of the present age. Hence the great weight of attention given in all religions to the *means* by which this precious information is preserved and made available to successive generations – the definition and interpretation of authoritative sources such as 'holy Scripture', the training and licensing of those authorized to teach and preach, the careful control of forms of worship which so often determine what people actually believe. Hence also that concern for bringing up children 'in the fear and nurture of the Lord' with which we began this discussion.

In the seventeenth century, as we saw, this system was beautifully simple – at least in theory. The sources from which children derived their religious education were strictly controlled: Church of England parents, Church of England schools, regular attendance at Church of England services, careful supervision of available reading matter. And this reflects a fundamental principle in the behaviour of systems: the more closed is the system, the easier it is to control and monitor the flow of information. A primitive tribal community is likely to be highly 'systematic' in its control of information. Rituals of life and death, standards of conduct, social conventions – all these will be unquestioningly inherited from the past and firmly inculcated in the next generation. So long as the tribe remains culturally isolated, or in contact at most with other tribes of a similar culture, the 'system' is likely to continue unchanged, generation after generation. But introduce a transistor radio, and the situation is radically changed. Suddenly there are members of the tribe who receive information from outside the system. Resources are suddenly available which are outside the control of the tribal institutions. The system is no longer a closed one; and if it is to survive it must either strengthen its boundaries by outlawing those who listen to transistors, or else adapt its procedures so as to make its own privileged information seem more valuable than that which can be derived from external sources. But by this process of adaptation it becomes a more open, and a more complex, system. The price that has to be paid for a greater openness to the world around is the loss of its original beautiful simplicity. To use the jargon of systems analysis, its members, instead of drawing only on the resources of their own culture and institutions, have become 'multiply resourceful'.

It is easy to see that something similar to this process

81

has taken place in the Church of England since the seventeenth century. Consider how an ordinary child is now brought up 'in the fear and nurture of the Lord'. His parents, still influenced by generations of church schooling, have probably decided that the task is better left to 'the professionals' – at most they will have inculcated some nursery prayers and some basic moral standards. They may also have sent the child along to Sunday School (if one still exists – somewhat against the prevailing fashion – in the parish), or have brought him regularly to parish communion; and the elementary instruction gained there may in a few cases have been continued in confirmation classes and resulted in a relatively informed and consolidated faith. But even at its best this church-based instruction will form a minute part of the child's education compared with what he receives at school. There, religious instruction takes a very small part of the day. The teacher may well be a member of a denomination other than the Church of England and may even not be a Christian. The lessons are likely to provide information on other faiths as well as Christianity. Most important of all, the emphasis (as in most of his education) is likely to fall on his own freedom to choose for himself. Different options will be described, different religions presented. The growing child is deliberately taught to be 'multiply resourceful'.

But let us take the ideal case. Let us suppose that the child, after surveying all this competing material, adheres firmly to his parents' faith, becomes a devout and committed confirmation candidate, and grows into a faithful member of the Church of England. Even then, his resources will by no means be limited to those provided by the system. He will be encouraged to use the bookstall, where many of the books will be by non-Anglicans (Michael Hollings or Anthony Bloom on prayer, George Macleod or Colin Morris on social

concern, C.H. Dodd or William Barclay on the Bible –
not an Anglican among them!). He may find his parish
committed to the ecumenical movement and hear
sermons by preachers from other denominations. He
may even find himself in dialogue with representatives
of other faiths – no longer now in order to refute them
or to demonstrate the superiority of Christianity, but in
the expectation of learning something new and authentic about God, about prayer, or about a religious life-
style. In short, he is actively encouraged, in his daily
church life as well as in his education, to become
'multiply resourceful'.

What does this say to us about the 'system' of the
church? It says, certainly, that the control and transmission of vital information in the church is a much
more complex matter than it was, say, when the Prayer
Book Catechism was written. But it also alerts us to a
very important feature of 'systems' in general. Every
system presupposes a boundary. To describe it at all,
you have to know what belongs to it and what does not.
That which lies within the system can be systematically
organized; that which lies outside may interact with the
system, but will obey different principles of organization. And more than this: where you draw the boundary
is to some extent a matter of choice. If you want to
study the efficiency of a particular factory, you may
draw a line round it and regard the factory itself as the
system to be analysed. But you may then find that
much that happens in the factory can be understood
only in the light of factors which impinge upon it from
outside, such as the state of the market, inflation, or
the availability of housing for workers in the area. You
may then find it preferable to regard the national eco-
nomy as the 'system', or perhaps the social pattern of
the area; the factory will then become a sub-system in a
larger system. In short, the boundary is not something

given; it can be drawn wherever it best suits you for the purpose of study.

This concept of shifting boundaries is clearly relevant to a study of the church. For certain purposes the Church of England is a self-contained system – even now, though more obviously in Reformation England, where it had fewer competitors and its members had a much narrower range of resources. It also contains sub-systems, such as a parish, a deanery, a diocese or a province: any of these may have means of circulating, transmitting and controlling information independently of the church as a whole. And there are sub-systems of other kinds, such as movements for Catholic Renewal or overseas Mission, which maintain themselves almost entirely by the systematic provision of information in the form of books, pamphlets, newssheets and visiting preachers or lecturers. But from another point of view the Church of England itself is part of a larger system – the Anglican Communion, the British Council of Churches, the Christian presence in this country, the family of the great religions in Britain today. It all depends on what you want to study. For certain purposes you can draw the boundary where you like.

And yet, in the case of religions and churches, there is an important sense in which it does matter where you draw the boundary. Indeed churches devote a good deal of attention and energy to what may be called 'boundary maintenance'. This is not true of all systems. A business, for example, may find it advantageous to merge with another and lose its separate identity – the boundaries may then be redrawn altogether; or it may preserve an operational identity for reasons of prestige and goodwill, like Harrods within the House of Fraser organization; in which case the boundaries, though less important, continue to be in place. But a church cannot afford to be casual about its own boundaries. The information which it offers it believes to be the truth, a truth vital to the well-being of its members and of mankind generally. It is essential that this truth should be carefully preserved and transmitted. It must not be distorted, diluted or added to without authorization. The greater part of this truth is held in common by all the main churches, which recognize each other as sub-systems within the wider system of the Christian presence in the world. The information provided by these churches will therefore be regarded as reliable within the system so far as the general truths of Christianity are concerned. But this will be the case only so long as it comes from within a certain boundary. Information provided by Christian Scientists, or Mormons, or Jehovah's Witnesses, may not be reliable at all; for these bodies lie outside the system, and the main Christian churches have an important responsibility to make clear where their boundary is drawn. This means that they have to offer some definition of who is a Christian and who is not; they have to impose some minimal conditions of membership (occasional church attendance, assent to certain doctrines, submission to baptism, etc.); and they have to specify the authoritative sources of their information (Scripture, tradition, Articles of Religion, etc.). All these matters require periodic revision and clarification. There is constant 'boundary maintenance' to be done in the matter of who is a Christian and who is not, what counts as a church, what sort of conduct and social organization (violent revolution, apartheid, certain forms of capitalism) is compatible with Christianity.

The churches also have an interest in maintaining their own denominational boundaries; but here the issues are a good deal more complex, and indeed their different attitudes to boundaries are one of the main factors of difference, and division, between the historic churches. At one end of the scale stands the Roman Catholic Church, with a clear policy on who counts as a member and who does not. Catholics are required to attend Mass regularly, to observe a certain discipline (in such matters as fasting, confession and birth control) and to show obedience to the teaching of the church as formulated from time to time by the Pope. Anyone who fails to observe these conditions may be reprimanded and subjected to the threat of exclusion from the sacraments; and no one can be a Catholic who has not been baptized or received into the Roman Catholic Church. At the other end of the scale stand those churches which feel free to put the words, 'All Welcome', on their notice boards, and to invite any stranger to take part in any of their services. Somewhere between the two (though perhaps nearer the second than the first) stands the Church of England, with its historic comprehensiveness, its willingness to offer baptism, marriage and funeral services on demand, and its disinclination to formulate strict rules for church membership.

It would be a mistake to imagine that this scale simply represents a greater or lesser concern with boundary maintenance as such. Even churches which make a point of welcoming visitors and strangers to their main services often have a criterion of membership which is more demanding even than that of the Roman Catholic Church. Anyone who begins to attend regularly will quickly be drawn into 'the fellowship', invited to receive instruction, and challenged to show that Christian 'commitment' which often characterizes congregations of this kind. The ethos of a strongly evangelical or charismatic church may often result in vigorous boundary maintenance; those who are not comfortable with it may feel themselves excluded and be virtually forced to leave, whereas a Roman Catholic who has difficulties with the church's traditional faith and discipline may receive considerable help from a parish priest and be encouraged to work through these difficulties over a long period. But it is probably true that, at least to outsiders, the Church of England appears to have more elusive boundaries, and to be more careless about boundary maintenance, than any other church. Is this really the case?

Before we try to answer this question there is one more point to be understood about boundaries themselves. They are not there just to contain and define a system, to show who is in and who is out. They also mark the point at which the system interacts with the outside world. It is possible, as we have seen, to think of a business enterprise as just a part of the economic system of this country: it affects, and is affected by, the rate of inflation, the tax laws, the price of world commodities and the state of the country's export drive. But for certain purposes it is also totally distinct from these things and requires a boundary which must be carefully maintained. In its dealings with the tax inspector, for example, it has the legal right to arrange its own affairs to its best advantage (within its constitution and the law of the land) and it will be careful to instruct its accountant about all the needs, the assets and the policies of the company. It will not allow him to regard the interests of the Inland Revenue as a determining factor in the policy of the company. In short, there must be no doubt on which side of the boundary the accountant stands: he is the company's man, not the tax man. But at the same time the Inland Revenue does have a considerable influence on the affairs of the company. The amount of tax payable on various operations is a factor in the choice between options. The accountant, who maintains this particular stretch of the boundary, requires full and authoritative information from the tax office;

he must be aware of relevant court decisions in recent tax cases; he must even know enough of the political scene to be able to forecast and provide against possible changes in the tax laws. His activity is strictly within the system of the company; but he cannot perform his task effectively without gaining information from outside.

It follows that boundary maintenance is not merely a matter of keeping the system intact; it is also a means of ensuring that the system is in touch with the rest of the world. The system can suffer from the boundary being too tightly drawn as much as it can from the boundary being indistinct. If the accountant's time is totally occupied with the internal efficiency of the company, a sudden recession or a change in the tax structure may take everyone by surprise and cause irreparable damage. If he is an outside consultant without adequate information about the company's internal structure he may be unaware of serious weaknesses within the system. What has to be decided is where he stands with relation to the boundary. If he is too far inside – too much the company's man – there is danger of one kind; if he is too far outside – too much the external consultant – there is danger of another kind. His actual position will be a kind of compromise – neither entirely in nor entirely out. And this will affect the boundary of the system at an important point. It must be maintained in a way that *both* protects the policy and interests of the company *and* keeps the necessary contacts open with the world outside. To the question, Is he part of the system?, there can be no neat answer. The boundary at this point is necessarily somewhat indistinct.

We are now in a better position to consider the apparently indistinct boundaries of the Church of England. That they *are* indistinct cannot be denied. We have already seen that in modern, 'multiply resourceful' society it is extremely difficult to control the information which enters any system, and that any Christian is bound to receive instruction in the faith from more than one source. But the Church of England seems to compound the difficulty by being remarkably vague about church membership. Who are members of the Church of England? Some would say, those who are baptized and confirmed, who attend worship regularly, play a part in parish life, make a substantial financial contribution, and are generally (as the modern expression goes) 'committed'. Others would say, anyone is a member who is prepared to write 'C. of E.' on a form; all English people have a legal right to bring their children to a Church of England church to be baptized, to solemnize their marriage in church (if they are baptized) and to be buried (if there is space) in the churchyard according to the rites and ceremonies of the Established Church. Others, again, would draw the line somewhere in between, to include, say, those who are on the Electoral Roll of a parish or who attend Communion on Easter Day, but to exclude those who merely claim membership without assuming any responsibility at all.

All these different approaches to 'boundary maintenance' have serious arguments to support them. Those on the stricter side will emphasize the gain to the church's influence and credibility if its members are all highly 'committed'. The church's witness will be clearer and sharper if church people are visibly serious about their faith. If almost anyone can call himself 'C. of E.', how can people be expected to know what the church stands for? On the other side it can be argued that, if it follows that road, the Church of England will rapidly become a 'sect', containing only like-minded people with a particularly high degree of commitment. What about all those other people who are still searching, who find occasional attendance a valuable stimulus and support, who value the church's continued existence even though they find it impossible to become deeply involved? What about the tremendous opportunities for influencing people to take Christianity seriously which are presented whenever a couple seeks a church wedding or a christening? What about the incalculable influence for good exercised on society by all those who, consciously or unconsciously, take their values and priorities from the church?

So the debate continues; and one point at least is clear. Wherever you draw the boundary, there will be losses as well as gains. For every new marker, a price has to be paid. If the boundary is too solid, the system may become remote from the world and fall victim to changes outside its control; if it is too indistinct, the system may cease to speak with a clear voice and runs the risk of falling apart. The recent history of the Roman Catholic Church is a case in point. Until less than twenty years ago, it had the most systematic structure and the clearest boundaries of any major church. Its organization was hierarchical and centralized, its teaching strictly controlled by authority, the books permitted to be read by its members were censored, the discipline imposed on all Catholics was strictly enforced, and the forms of worship were uniform (in Latin) throughout the world. The strengths of this system were immense, but the price paid was a degree of isolation from the rest of the world which, by the 'sixties, had become a serious danger to survival. And so, at Vatican II, the boundaries were loosened and blurred. Members of other Christian denominations were recognized as a kind of associate member of the true church. Rules for belonging (with respect to attendance at Mass, fasting, sacramental confession, marriage with non-Roman Catholic partners) were relaxed. Many kinds of contacts with the non-Catholic world were opened up. The gain from these changes has been immense: the danger of becoming an inward-looking, almost sectarian, church has been averted. But the price paid has been heavy. The Catholic way of life is no longer so distinct. Catholics profess allegiance to the Pope, but disobey his teaching over birth-control. Their own conscience, more than the directives of their priests, dictates many aspects of their religious observance. They draw their information from many sources. Like everyone else, they have become 'multiply resourceful'. As a result, their church has lost the power of a uniform message and practice. In certain areas, at least, its boundaries have become indistinct.

But if there is loss as well as gain in any adjustment of the boundaries, there is still greater loss in giving in completely to either side of the argument. It is here that this whole approach of 'systems analysis' may help individual church members to understand their own role in the Church of England. We must not, of course, claim too much for this approach. The Church of England may be in some respects a 'system'; but it certainly is not in all respects. Systems exist to provide certain goods and services; they have objects to attain, standards of efficiency to conform to. The church, by contrast, exists for the praise of God and the service of men and women; and no 'systems analysis' is necessarily going to help us to do either of these things better. Yet we do find in the church certain features which are shared by other systems; and we do find tensions and arguments going on which relate to what might be called boundaries and boundary maintenance. It is reasonable to think that understanding systems may help us to understand better at least certain aspects of church life.

We saw at the outset that a necessary feature of any system is the control and transmission of information, and that this is true to a high degree of the church, which claims to offer information that is vital for salvation. An

91

important concern, therefore, for church members must be to make sure that this task – the transmission of reliable and authentic information – is effectively performed. Now this information comes in the main from the distant past. It has been the responsibility of the Church down the ages to ensure that it is made available to each successive generation in the purest and most faithful form possible. At various times Christians have disagreed about how this should best be done. Should it be by means of a strictly authorized class of teachers in the Church, the 'clergy'? Or should it be through the personal attention of all church members to Scripture, some form of regular and official 'Bible study'? Such disagreements have occasionally been so profound that they have led to divisions in the Church – the two points of view just mentioned contributed to the emergence of 'Catholic' and 'Protestant' positions at the Reformation. But, whatever position was taken, all were agreed on the fundamental importance of the task. The faith must be handed on, and this requires a clear system. We must know who is authorized to preach and teach, we must know who professes the faith and who does not, the boundary must be clearly drawn, the system must be strong enough to maintain the reliability and authenticity of the message of salvation.

So far so good. But the Church does not exist only for its own members. It has a message for the world, a service to offer to mankind. It cannot afford to get out of touch with society. There must be constant interaction at the frontiers, constant reinterpretation of the sacred information, a constant movement back and forth across the boundaries. This is a work which cannot be guaranteed by the structures of the system. It depends on the initiative and enterprise of individuals, some of whom are neither in nor out. It involves sending out explorers whose links with their base may become strained and tenuous. It runs the risk of nurturing adventurers who will become critical of their home base. It will create tension between those who reach across the boundaries and those committed to boundary maintenance. It may even seem at times like a conflict between the individual and the institution.

We asked earlier on whether the Church of England devotes sufficient attention to its boundaries, whether it keeps its system in good repair. The result of this comparison with other organizations and institutions is that we can perhaps see more clearly how to answer this question. It is often claimed that the Church of England is 'both Catholic and Reformed'. One of the implications of this claim is that it is continually exposed to the tension between boundary maintenance and boundary transcendence. It has a deep concern for the faithful transmission of the authentic information required for salvation; hence the store it sets by its continuity from the early days of Christianity, guaranteed by its apostolic ministry and its constant attention to Scripture and creeds. But it also has a concern to adapt to the needs of the present, to reach out into every sphere of society, to offer a welcome and a chance for reflection and Christian maturing to people who are far from feeling committed to the faith. Most of us can probably recognize ourselves on one side or the other of this debate; many of us may feel the tension within ourselves. We may often feel rebellious and frustrated, either because the church does not seem to be taking its historic heritage seriously enough, or because it is not sufficiently open to new forms and new ideas. But the vital thing to recognize is that both concerns are necessary if the church is to live and flourish. It would be disastrous if either were to prevail over the other; it would be equally disastrous if there were no tension between them. Each of us has a part to play in fostering that aspect of the 'system' with which we feel most affinity. We can all be actively involved in either maintaining or transcending boundaries. But we must also ensure that the church we belong to continues to be one where both are possible, and where the tension between the two continues to be a sign of life, of seriousness about God and of openness to the world.

7
Learning the Language

Visitors to Taizé, the ecumenical community in France, are sometimes startled by the apparent contrast between the monastery and its visitors. On the one hand is a community of monks, practising an austere and disciplined life, conducting their worship according to traditional forms, and for the most part inaccessible to outsiders. On the other is a huge stream of visitors, mainly young people, many of whom would acknowledge no particular Christian allegiance, and some of whom would actually call themselves atheists. Yet three times a day the church is crowded with these visitors, joining in the worship and remaining for long periods in silent contemplation. Normally, people attend church services because they are 'practising Christians', for whom regular worship is an obligation deliberately, and often gladly, taken on. But many of these young people have no association with the Church whatever, and certainly have not yet accepted either the Christian faith or Christian standards of moral and social conduct. What brings them to Taizé? And why do they take part in the daily worship if they do not yet believe?

In part they are drawn by the sheer beauty of the worship; the numinous interior of the church, with its icons, its flickering candles and simple images and symbols; the informality combined with reverence; the vigorous and well-disciplined singing and the superb organ music; the mixture of traditional liturgical forms with prayers that are sensitive to the needs of people all over the world; the evident sincerity and naturalness of the Brothers, and the frankness and readiness to listen of those they are able to meet; the sense of commitment to church unity, social justice and human solidarity on an international scale; the exhilaration of sharing with like-minded people from all over the world. But along with all this goes a factor which makes Taizé unlike any other church – indeed it is not a 'church' at all. It is simply a monastic community which conducts its worship in public, welcomes all who wish to attend, and offers hospitality and service to its visitors so far as it can without seriously disrupting its own life. It makes no demands – other than practical and domestic ones. Visitors are asked to show consideration to residents, to observe silence at certain times, to adopt a certain pattern of activity for the day or for the week. But beyond that, there is no 'commitment' whatever. People may come and go believing what they please, professing what they please, and fashioning their lives as they please. No obligations are imposed, no questions asked. In short, there is total freedom. Every individual is accepted on his or her own terms. There is no pressure to conform. And it is this, among other things, that draws young people in their thousands.

Many, of course, may go to Taizé, and many more may leave it, much more 'committed' than this. Some are active Christians before they go there, others become so during their stay. Friendships and loyalties are formed which influence subsequent conduct, informal Christian instruction and advice is available, and many people find their faith enlarged and deepened after a few days' exposure to the worship, the discussions and the sense of participation in a world-wide movement. Yet Taizé proclaims with great emphasis that it is *not* a movement, it is *not* a church. Its only intention is that its visitors may return to their homes, their work-places, their parishes and churches with a new vision and a new determination. Visitors to Taizé are not thought of as potential recruits to an organization, potential supporters of a movement, potential converts. They are all *searchers*, engaged in mankind's universal quest for knowledge and experience of God. Anyone may come, nothing is demanded. All that is offered is a welcome, and the opportunity to share in the search in whatever way is right for oneself.

Many churches whose members have visited Taizé find themselves wondering why they cannot exercise the same attraction themselves. They may even adopt certain features of what they take to be a Taizé 'style' – Gelineau-type psalm-singing, informal sitting around on carpets and stools instead of regimented pews or chairs, long periods of silence in worship. These things often do make worship more attractive, especially to young people. But they cannot alter a fundamental difference between Taizé and any church whatever. Taizé, we have seen, is not a church. It has no members (other than its own monks), it makes no demands. People may come and go, but they cannot belong. No restrictions are placed on them, they can believe what they please, they can come and go as they please. They can infer from the liturgy, from books and pamphlets published at Taizé, and from conversations with the Brothers, what the Community believes. They may find it a legitimate and powerful expression of the historic faith of Christendom. But they remain absolutely free to accept or reject, to agree or disagree, to be persuaded or repelled. There are no claims, no commitments, no pressure. The searching spirit may blow where it listeth.

No church can offer this freedom; in one sense, therefore, no church can be so 'attractive'. Or perhaps we should say rather that a church offers an attraction of a different kind. All of us, at one time or another in our lives, require a period in which we may search for the truth about God and ourselves in perfect freedom. We are not ready, we say, to be 'committed'. We need to keep our options open, to make our religious explorations without incurring obligations to anyone. This may be a necessary stage. But it is equally true that we cannot prolong it indefinitely. Our freedom will have been of no use to us if we never come to a decision. At some stage, if we are to live a full and satisfying life, we have to take the plunge and commit ourselves to a religion, an ideology, a party, a style of conduct and action. When we do so, we shall of course lose some of our freedom. Our beliefs and behaviour will now be determined, to a greater or lesser extent, by the group or society to which we have chosen to belong. Within that group or society we shall now have opportunities for responsible action, service and companionship which were not available so long as we preserved our total freedom. We shall probably find these opportunities more satisfying, and shall not regret those options we are no longer free to adopt. Having used our freedom to hesitate long between, say, Christianity and Marxism, and having finally opted for Christianity, we shall not regret that we have now lost the freedom to consider becoming a Marxist. Indeed we may find that the more limited freedom we now have to fashion our lives within the bounds imposed by Christian morality is more satisfying than the freedom we had before to follow any morality we chose.

The Church, at any rate, represents an option. If you choose to belong, you forfeit some of your freedom. You can no longer believe what you like and do what you like. Consequently the Church can never be attractive, as Taizé is attractive, to those who are at the stage of requiring total freedom for their religious quest. But at the same time there are degrees of freedom and degrees of commitment. For some, a church may be attractive because it offers precise instruction in matters of belief and authoritative guidance in matters of conduct. For others, the decision to join a church may be easier if there is freedom to work out one's own faith and reach one's own decisions within general guidelines. Churches do in fact differ in the extent to which they encourage or limit the freedom of the individual, and one way to discover what a church believes is to see what claims it makes upon its members and how much freedom of belief and conscience it allows them.

Suppose then that someone who is seriously considering the option of the Christian religion (perhaps after a visit to Taizé) brings himself to approach a church. How will he be received? What demands will be made of him? It is probably safe to say that in many parish churches in this country no notice will be taken of him at all! He may simply find himself, as an anonymous member of the congregation, trying to find his way through a complicated service that is unfamiliar to him, and being invited only to give some money for the collection. As a matter of fact, this may be exactly what he wants. He may not be ready for a group of Christian people to seize him warmly by the hand, assuming he is one of them. He may want to know more about it, to get the feel of it, before becoming in any way involved. And this he can do, simply by coming to church Sunday by Sunday. It is rather like getting to know the language of a family. All families have their own private stories, private jokes, private assumptions. However warmly a stranger is welcomed, he will go on feeling a stranger until he has learnt this 'family language' and come to understand and share the history and the feelings it expresses. In the same way, a stranger in church has to learn a new language. To become more fully a member, he needs to get used to the way the church organizes itself when addressing God, how it talks about the world, what assumptions its members share. And simply attending services is for many the best way of doing so.

It is worth exploring the 'family language' analogy a little further. There exist associations, clubs, and societies in which a new member is obliged to declare his acceptance of the rules, or his assent to a set of principles and beliefs, before he can join. This is clearly a very different procedure from that of joining a family circle. A newcomer to a family is not usually asked to subscribe to that family's beliefs or bind himself to their standards of conduct before he can be accepted. If he finds that the family in question has views or beliefs which he did not know about at first – if, for instance, they turn out to be shockingly racist or aggressively enthusiastic Jehovah's Witnesses – then he will have to make a decision whether he can continue to be closely associated with them; and the more he learns their 'family language' the clearer it will become whether their whole system of attitudes and beliefs is one that he can wholeheartedly accept or one that alienates them from him.

It is clear that joining the Church of England (or indeed most churches) is more like joining a family than joining an association which has strict rules for admission. The first requirement is to learn the language. Much of this – Scripture, psalms and hymns – is shared with most churches. Some – the style of preaching, and of informal intercessions and prayers – is more specifically Anglican. And particular nuances may be found in those sources of a common language which are the particular possession of the Church of England: the Book of Common Prayer and the Alternative Service Book. As the stranger grows familiar with these things, he begins to become aware of the beliefs and attitudes they express. He gradually learns the faith of the church and its spiritual and moral demands; in a word, he discovers 'what the church believes'. As he does so, he either feels increasingly alienated, in which case he will cease to attend, or he will feel more at home, beginning to sense that this is the 'family' he wants to belong to.

But belonging to a family means more than just listening to its conversation. It means sharing its joys and sorrows, taking part in common tasks and assuming a family loyalty. In due course – sooner in some churches, later in others – the stranger will be noticed by the vicar or by members of the congregation and invited to join in parish activities. Questions are unlikely to be asked about his religious beliefs. It will simply be assumed that, since he attends church, he is in sympathy with what 'church' stands for, and will regard traditional church activities, social gatherings, Bible study, money-raising, etc., as an appropriate consequence of church attendance. Here is another point at which he may feel alienated. Just as the stranger in a family may begin to find this family's favourite pursuits not to his taste, and so may prefer to break off the connection, so our new church member may feel ill at ease with parish activities. He may recognize that such activities are in fact implied by Christian faith; but as a result he may begin to wonder whether the Christian faith is right for him. He may, for instance, find himself doubting (after some parish get-together) whether he is capable of loving his neighbour quite so indiscriminately as Jesus seems to demand. Or he may simply be shrinking from the loss of personal freedom which these new commitments imply, and realize that he simply was not ready to accept the constraints that are involved in belonging to an active organization. But equally, he may find the activities which are proposed for him natural and congenial; then, as he takes part in them, he will get to know the family better and deepen his understanding of the convictions and principles which animate its members.

In all this, nothing has been said about any explicit discussion of Christian belief. This may of course come up at quite an early stage. Our enquirer may be a person who has never been baptized or confirmed, has had little Christian teaching in school and no opportunity subsequently to learn the elements of Christianity. If so, he will doubtless be encouraged to offer himself for baptism and confirmation, and this will involve some course of instruction. But he could equally well be someone who was baptized, or even confirmed, in childhood, and who has all his life had some slight knowledge of the essentials of the Christian faith. If so, he is perhaps more likely to find the church trying to involve him in practical Christian work than asking questions about his beliefs. Many church members go through their entire adult lives without ever having to give an account of precisely what they believe – which in fact, as we saw in the first chapter of this book, they would probably be unable to do. It is simply assumed that through long habituation they will have so soaked up the church's 'family language' that their beliefs and attitudes will by now have set firmly in a Church of England mould. It is this silent and almost unconscious acceptance of what is said and heard in church which often makes it so difficult to answer the question, 'What does the Church believe?' A large number of church members have never had to ask the question of themselves.

But let us suppose that our new member attends an adult confirmation class, and that the church to which he has attached himself contains lively study groups for Bible reading and the discussion of the faith. Certainly these activities will bring doctrinal questions into the open. He, along with others, will be challenged to work out what he believes. But he may also find that these sessions seem remarkably 'non-directive'. Discussions may range widely, a variety of views may be expressed, and he may be sent home to do some more reading and thinking that will help him towards a true Christian understanding. No one seems over-anxious that he should fall into line or declare himself soundly orthodox, and when the day comes when he is confirmed and identifies himself with the Church, only the most general statement of belief is demanded of him. On a great many matters his position is left to his own judgement and conscience – and no one else seems greatly concerned.

Or does no one? Let us think for a moment of the other actors in the drama. The bishop, who presides at the confirmation, has the responsibility of preserving sound doctrine in the church. The parish priest, who has prepared every candidate presented to the bishop, has the responsibility of making sure that they are properly grounded in the Christian faith. Other members of the congregation, who may have shared in discussions with the candidate, could have noticed if he seems badly at sea over any particular matter. All these people are concerned that the true faith should be preserved and transmitted, that the church should be faithful to its inheritance and that no scandal should be given by its members. The question is, how this concern is expressed. New members are not given a complete checklist of doctrines they must subscribe to on admission. Rather it is a matter of helping them in any way that is possible to make their own the family language of the church, and to do so with integrity and understanding.

Let us take the analogy one stage further. Not all families are happy and united. They have quarrels and estrangements – but still a basic family loyalty may persist. Not all family members live together. Some may live in a far country, and the family language which enables those at home to communicate with each other instantly and easily may need many more words of explanation if it is to be intelligible to those who have drifted out of touch. Families may have their black sheep, members who rebel against the family ethos and yet come back again and again to renew contact. In all these respects the analogy still fits. The Church of England has family differences in abundance, but a basic loyalty keeps it together. It has members who seem at best loosely attached, and are barely aware of the slowly changing language of the church, but who nevertheless will rally to the cause, if their cherished beliefs and institutions seem threatened, by unexpectedly appearing at church meetings or even writing letters to *The Times*. It has black sheep – persons often of great enthusiasm and integrity, deeply attached to the Christian faith but determined to see things and do things in their own way, and causing considerable disturbance each time they reappear. All these can be held, even if with difficulty, within the family. All contribute to its language – that is, to its believing. All are manifestations of the phenomenon with which we began this chapter: the interplay of the freedom of the individual with the constraint and commitment involved in belonging to the church.

But now we must look at it from the point of view of the church. How open and welcoming can a church afford to be? Can it really accept anyone as a member so long as he or she is an honest enquirer, ready to suspend judgement on a number of important matters until the mysterious ethos of the Church of England gradually seeps into heart and mind? Is there not a danger that it may lose hold of vital truths unless it proclaims clearly the doctrines which must be accepted by every member? This certainly was the motive of the great revivals of the eighteenth and nineteenth centuries. Some felt that without a stricter hold upon the sacramental side of church life and a stronger discipline of spiritual life people were hardly being serious about their Christianity. Others saw the greatest weakness of the church in a lack of evangelical fervour, and created a climate of church life in which only those committed to the explicit proclamation of their religion would feel comfortable. It seemed and still seems to many churchpeople that there are certain Christian truths which must be held on to, come what may, and that no one can be accepted in the family of the church who has serious doubts about them. It is, after all, on matters of doctrine that Christians have differed most violently from each other even to the point of putting one another to death. Would it not be a sign of a sick and irresolute church if assent to these truths ceased to be a condition of membership?

All this is certainly true. The church is entrusted with truth, and has an absolute obligation to preserve that truth and pass it on to subsequent generations. The only way it can do so is by ensuring that its members believe this truth and live faithfully by it. On some matters, it would seem, no compromise is possible. 'If you don't believe that', it may say, 'you can't belong.' And yet this apparently sensible view of the church collides with the awkward fact that you cannot actually *compel* people to believe anything. What an individual does or does not believe is a highly personal matter. If someone has difficulties with the Virgin Birth or the resurrection of the body you can argue and plead but you cannot force. *That I can't believe* was the title of the sequel which Bishop Robinson wrote to his *Honest to God.* They were not the words of an imaginary non-Christian, trying to pour ridicule on the teaching of the Church. They were intended to be taken as a kind of plea for help uttered by a serious believer who was feeling real difficulties of conscience in accepting certain traditional doctrines taught by the Church. Indeed, many would say that the main service performed by Bishop Robinson through these books was that of enabling church members to bring out into the open the difficulties of belief they were experiencing without feeling there was a risk of censure or expulsion. There may be many occasions on which it is right for any church to define its faith and to say what it believes. But it is quite another matter for it to make explicit assent to its doctrines a formal condition of membership. Church members are all individuals. They are all working out their faith, they are all seeking to follow Christ and to bring their lives into conformity with his teaching. The doctrine taught by the Church provides the necessary framework; and people belong to a particular church because by and large they find the framework is a help rather than a hindrance to the practice and growth of their personal religion. The moment acceptance of a particular doctrine is demanded of every member, the church becomes a sect of like-minded people, instead of a community of infinitely varied men and women worshipping God, serving their neighbours and advancing like a close-knit and loyal team of variously gifted explorers towards the great and ineffable mystery of God.

The result of all this, of course, is tension. Just as a trade union or a political party requires absolute solidarity from its members if it is going to achieve its ends, and yet must encourage new ideas and differences of opinion if it is to remain a living force, so the church, like any other institution, requires its members to stand together against the attacks and challenges of the secular world, and yet at the same time must encourage discussion, debate and new thinking in the interpretation of its historic teaching and in the application of the Christian gospel to the modern world. Much of this inevitable tension lies behind those party differences which so regrettably (in the eyes of many) divide, not only the Church of England, but many other provinces of the Anglican Communion. Many will say (for example) that you cannot be a Christian without confessing Christ as your 'personal saviour'. Others follow the slogan, 'It's the Mass that matters', and believe that every other expression of Christian living and piety is secondary to the observance of the sacramental tradition of the church. Each of these beliefs goes along with a definite position in the Church of England, and those who take them most seriously cannot but believe that everyone else in the church ought to accept them wholeheartedly. If they did not believe this, they would be failing in their witness to what they see as an important aspect of the Christian faith. But there will always be other people in the Church of England who find these propositions impossible to accept. They may find the words 'my personal saviour' inappropriate or even meaningless; they may be unable to accept that the Eucharist, however important, should be given such exclusive priority. These people are not to be cold-shouldered or expelled by their more dogmatic brethren. They may be taking their church membership and Christian discipleship extremely seriously, and find the 'family language' of the Church of England one with which they feel at home. They cannot accept that they are less 'Christian' than their Evangelical or Anglo-catholic fellow-Anglicans. There is an inevitable tension here. It need not – we pray it will not always – be reinforced by Evangelical and Catholic party groupings in the church. But a certain conflict is bound to exist between, on the one hand, the need to state clearly and definitely 'what we believe', and, on the other hand, the freedom of the individual to find his own way to his own personal faith. Where the conflict is recognized,

and allowed to promote reflection and deeper understanding, then it is a healthy sign of 'believing in the
church'.

8
Standing Outside

'I have just returned from a sabbatical period in India. I was there for four months, just wandering around and talking with many different people of many different faiths, and going into their places of worship and talking with them, and this was a remarkable experience. I do commend it . . . as a way of standing outside oneself a little bit and coming back at problems from a slightly different angle.'

This is an extract from a speech made by a lay member of General Synod during a debate in 1983. In general terms it was perhaps a very obvious thing to say. Foreign travel may be good for all of us; it widens our perspectives, and makes us less parochial and insular in our outlook. But the context in which his remark was made gave it more significance. It was in the course of a debate on whether redundant churches should be made available to adherents of other faiths. Strongly opposing views had already been expressed, resting upon deep Christian convictions. It was then that this speaker argued that things may look different if one has an opportunity to travel, to make personal contact with other religions, and so to 'stand outside oneself a little bit'.

This invitation to 'stand outside' one's own religion and culture is a new phenomenon so far as Christianity is concerned. In the early days of the Christian religion the attitude to other religions was exactly as it had been in the Jewish religion. The only other type of religion which was ever encountered was 'idolatry', that is, the worship of images of a variety of 'gods', whether in the

109

Baal-worship of Mesopotamian cultures or the paganism of the Greco-Roman world. It was occasionally admitted that some supernatural or occult power might reside in these pagan deities – Paul seems to concede this when he speaks of 'demons' inhabiting idols (1 Cor. 10.20); and it was often realized that, in pagan religion, it was not the statues themselves that were worshipped but the gods and goddesses they were thought to represent. But the reaction of Jews, as of Christians after them, to the temples and statues of pagan deities which they saw in profusion in every Greek or Roman city in the Empire was that all this was an abominable perversion of the worship of the one true God. Of course, in the Old Testament as in the New, there is occasional recognition that God may make himself known to other peoples, and even through other religions and philosophies. Nevertheless, the notion of 'standing outside oneself' and of actually learning something about God from pagans would have made no sense whatever to either Jews or Christians. 'Idolatry' was to be fought and ridiculed with every means at one's disposal.

As Christianity, within the very first decades of its existence, began to detach itself from Judaism, its attitude to this 'other faith' became increasingly hostile and polemical. It is clear from the New Testament that there had been considerable persecution, or at least harassment, of Christians by Jews in the early years; but it was not long before the increasing numbers and influence of the Christians reversed the situation, and the history of the Church up to quite recent times has included many deplorable episodes of anti-semitism, persecution and humiliation of the Jews. These were the people who had failed to understand their own divinely-inspired Scriptures, who had failed to recognize the Messiah when he came, and who had committed the ultimate crime of 'deicide' in condemning Jesus to

110

death. Again, any idea of entering into their religious experience and learning from them would have been inconceivable. It was only in the seventeenth century that Christian scholars began to recognize that learned Jews might have something useful to tell them about the Hebrew language and the meaning of certain passages in the Old Testament (even though St Jerome had done the same over a thousand years before). And it is only in the last few years that serious dialogues have got going between Christians and Jews, each respecting the convictions and integrity of the other.

The only other major religion with which Christians had any frequent contact before modern times was Islam. But this was contact of a kind extremely unfavourable to any mutual appreciation and understanding. The advance of a Muslim Arab empire into Christian lands, from the Ummayad conquest of Jerusalem in the seventh century to the siege of Vienna by the Ottomans in the seventeenth, was a threat to which Christian Europe was constantly exposed and which was finally eliminated only with the extinction of the Ottoman Empire in the First World War. Throughout this time all Muslims were, by definition, enemies. Their religion denied the divinity, and even the crucifixion, of Jesus Christ. They were 'infidels', apparently committed to the spread of their religion by force of arms. The occasional magnanimity and tolerance of a leader such as Suleiman, seldom equalled by Christian generals in their treatment of Muslims, was grudgingly acknowledged; but that any serious attention should be given by Christians to the Muslim religion as such remained inconceivable until quite recent times. Even historians were slow to recognize the immense debt which European culture owes to Arab art, philosophy and science; and serious dialogue between the two faiths is a very modern phenomenon indeed.

The next opportunity for contact with other religions was created by the great missionary movement which followed the extension of European trade and territorial claims into other continents from the seventeenth century onwards, and which reached its climax in the formation of powerful and well-funded missionary societies in the nineteenth century. Far the greatest success was achieved by these missionaries in Africa. Here, the indigenous religions they encountered seemed patently to be part of the primitive culture they had come to enlighten and educate. Tribal animism, ancestor-worship, witch-doctors: all these seemed a modern replica of the pagan idolatry which is so bitterly attacked in the Bible. The conversion of these lost souls to the true Light of the World presented itself as an urgent task to Christian consciences in Europe, and was often a remarkably fruitful enterprise: substantial parts of Africa became, and have remained, predominantly Christian. In other parts of the world, where other 'major faiths' had long been established, the story was rather different. In India, the Christian gospel made little headway except among those who, because of their caste, were virtually excluded from the benefits of their own religion and culture; and in Egypt, even such a devoted and sympathetic missionary as Temple Gairdner had to admit that the prospects of making converts in a Muslim society were extremely slender. In short, none of these great missionary enterprises was such as to encourage Christians to pay serious attention to the religious beliefs and practices of the people with whom they came in contact.

In the last half-century a very great change has come over Christian missionary strategy. In part, this has been the result of the end of the colonial era. The spread of Christianity in Africa (and to a lesser extent in India and the Far East) was in part a consequence of imperialism.

With the imposition of European administration, culture and trading patterns went the establishment of Christian schools and hospitals and the inculcation of Christian moral standards. With the end of empire and the beginning of independence such importations, however much they had been valued in the past, ceased to be welcome. Missionaries could no longer claim the right to 'Christianize' these countries; at most, they could continue their work in hospitals, schools and existing Christian congregations, trusting that the quality of their service would amount to a continuing witness to their faith and bring people to Christ, given that a more vigorous and explicit style of evangelism was no longer open to them. With this change of circumstances went a change in theological thinking. 'Mission' began to be understood, not so much as preaching and converting, but more as humble *service* to others in the name of Christ. And this involved, for the first time, a readiness to listen, carefully and sympathetically, to the religious beliefs and presuppositions of those among whom they worked.

This change of strategy and understanding has not been immediately grasped by the wider Christian public in this country. The old stereotype of the missionary with a Bible in one hand and an umbrella in the other dies hard. School children are still tempted to put a trouser button in the collection plate when the collection is for 'foreign missions'. They sense, correctly, that it may no longer be appropriate to try to 'convert the heathen'. But they may not yet have been made aware that this is no longer the programme which missionary societies are promoting. Still less has the new attitude of missionaries towards other world faiths made an impact on the thinking of the majority of European Christians. But meanwhile another factor has emerged which affects us all far more directly: immigration. The movement of populations has changed the religious and cultural map of Europe to an extent undreamt of a short time ago. Berlin is now the largest Turkish city in the world after Ankara and Istanbul. There are far more Muslims from Pakistan in Britain today than there have ever been Jews. Hindu and Sikh temples are being built in a number of English cities. 'Relations with other faiths' is no longer an issue to be faced by missionaries overseas. It has become a matter of everyday concern for Christians in many parts of Britain.

What sort of issue is this? On the face of it, it is plainly theological. Christian theology stresses the universality of our religion. Jesus appears to have made total and unrestricted claims: 'No one comes to the Father but by me' (John 14.6). The Christian revelation embodies the truth about God; by definition, therefore, every other religion must be false, at least in so far as it differs from Christianity. All this seems implicit in Christian doctrine and it has been held without question by theologians for centuries. But greater awareness of other world religions, brought about by much more frequent contact with their adherents, has introduced some new and insistent questions. Are there not followers of other faiths whose zeal, discipline of prayer and experience of God put the majority of our fellow-Christians to shame? Is it realistic, or even desirable, to think that the whole world could ever be converted to Christianity, and would it be a better place (given the record of 'Christian' nations) if it were? Is not Christianity itself deeply affected by the European culture in which it has chiefly flourished, and may not other 'ways to God' be more appropriate to peoples whose historical and cultural background is totally different from ours? In this increasingly secular and materialistic world, may it not be better to have some religion than none?

These are indeed theological questions, and theologians

have begun to take them very seriously. If one looks at some recent attempts to expound the Christian faith, such as Hans Küng's *On Being a Christian*, one finds that the argument is no longer confined to the Christian revelation alone: it is recognized at the outset that you cannot now make a credible case for Christianity without taking into account the fact that the majority of the world's population, if they find their way to God at all, do so through some religion other than Christianity. Yet the question remains an extremely difficult one. It is tempting, of course, to think of Christianity as just one of the paths up a mountain at the top of which we shall all have the ultimate vision of God; some will even say that, in the end, all religions 'come to the same thing'. On the other hand, there is an 'all or nothing' character about Christianity. The revelation of God in Jesus Christ seems incapable of being offered just as one of the possible options available to men and women in their religious quest. There is a sense in which Christianity claims, and must claim, to be *true*. And it makes no sense to say that something is true unless one is thereby ready to admit that certain other things are false. Moreover, there are moral as well as doctrinal issues involved. Christians may find themselves recoiling from public executions promoted by a Muslim regime in Teheran, from the self-immolation of Buddhist monks in Asia, or from the fatalistic attitude to human suffering often characteristic of Islam.

There are no easy answers to these questions. Theologians are now wrestling with them with a new sense of urgency, and have already proposed certain 'models' which may help to resolve these difficulties. In this country, one of the most influential has been that suggested by Professor John Hick, according to which the reality of God is necessarily experienced from the vantage point of one particular religion, but each of these religions themselves must be thought of as a kind of satellite circling at a different distance from the ultimate reality of God, each having only a partial vision of his totality. This, in turn, raises theological difficulties, and the enquiry will doubtless continue for many years to come. But it is the argument of this book that on a matter of this kind the belief of the Church does not and cannot depend only on the work of theologians. We have already seen how the accidents of history have influenced the attitude of Christians, and consequently the teaching of the Church, about other world religions. We must now give an example of the ways in which the same thing is happening today. We shall find that individual church members have as important a part to play in this area of Christian doctrine as in any other.

How will they do this? Here, the quotation with which we began this chapter becomes highly relevant. English people are not well prepared by their history or their religion to take seriously the beliefs and customs of other races. To do so, they need to 'stand outside themselves a little bit'. Indeed much will depend on their approach to ethnic minorities in general. It is often noticed that those British people who show least respect to their West Indian or Asian neighbours, and find it hard to think of them as playing anything but a menial and subservient role in British society, are those who have had no opportunity to travel and who never go further afield for their holidays than Brighton or Bournemouth. The reason is that they have never had an opportunity to see black or coloured people occupying distinguished positions and performing responsible tasks in their own countries, and have therefore received no challenge to a kind of instinctive European belief that these people are in some way inferior to themselves. By contrast, those who have travelled more widely, or who in one way or another have had a chance to converse on

equal terms with people from Asia, Africa or the Carib-
bean, find it comparatively easy to accept them and
respect them, and are much more ready to take seriously the moral and social standards and conventions
which these people have inherited from their cultural
and religious backgrounds. And so it is with religion.
Those Christians who have no experience whatever of
the worship and spirituality of other faiths may unconsciously dismiss all other religions as primitive or insigni-
ficant. But anyone who has seen the area round an
important mosque (such as the Haram surrounding the
El Aqsa Mosque and the Dome of the Rock in Jerusalem)
completely covered by bodies prostrate in prayer, or
has had experience of oriental techniques of meditation,
will be bound to approach his Muslim or Hindu neighbours in a more positive and respectful way.

Much will depend, therefore, on an initial readiness
to take other religions seriously. Thereafter, things may
go slowly. In many parts of England Christians may
have virtually no opportunity for contact with people of
other faiths, and the question, if thought about at all,
will remain theoretical. But others may be confronted
with it in a sharp form. The head teacher of a C. of E.
school in an inner city area may find that the majority
of his pupils are Muslims, Sikhs or Hindus. But he is
bound by law to conduct 'Assembly', which is supposed
to be a form of Christian worship and prayer. What does
he do? The leader of a youth club started by the parish
church may find that almost all the boys have another
religious background; but it is supposed to be a 'Christian' club, closing each night with a few moments of
prayer. Again, what is he to do? He will hardly turn to
the works of Professor John Hick: his problem is not
the theological relationship of the major world faiths.
And if he turns to the local authorities of his own
church, he is not likely to get a very helpful answer: the
problem is a new one, and accepted guidelines have not

yet been established. In the end he will have no option but to trust his own good sense, to work out his own policy, and to learn so far as he can from his own experience. He may of course take the line of least resistance, and simply utter some vaguely religious words for the sake of form. But if he is himself a sincere and practising Christian he will want to do more than this. He will consult with local clergymen and friends; he will take trouble to learn more about the religion of the children; and he will not be afraid to make mistakes if in so doing he can learn how best to be true to his own faith while respecting that of others.

This example is by no means fictional; such things have been happening in a number of cities in England. Let us now take it a stage further. Suppose our teacher or youth club leader, after patient experiment, begins to find a style of prayer which seems appropriate. It may be one which is very general and non-committal: he may feel that his children would be unable to join in anything which had a specifically Christian sound. Or he may find that he gains their respect precisely by refusing to compromise with his own beliefs and by allowing them to express theirs. We assume that he has been sharing his difficulties and questions with others in the church; he will also presumably share with them such success as he believes he has obtained. It may then happen that other Christians in the area find themselves in similar situations. It will be natural for them to be referred to him for advice. And he may even find that his influence begins to spread further. The General Synod, for instance, may have set up a commission to deal with this very subject. The local bishop may have recommended him to serve on it in view of his creative work in this field. In the commission (as we saw in an earlier chapter) he will find himself in company with theologians and other 'experts', whose thinking he may influence as much as he is influenced by theirs. His voice will then have become one among the many which are listened to in the attempt to answer the question, What (in this particular matter) does the church believe?

The later stages of this little story are of course imaginary. The situation described, though it occurs, is an exceptional one, and the Church of England has not yet officially tackled its implications. But the scenario is by no means unreal. Indeed (as I have tried to show) this is exactly how things do happen in the church, and it would not be at all surprising if the issue has to be dealt with in this way in a few years' time. Nevertheless, the majority of church members are unlikely to find themselves in a situation of this kind. Have they therefore no part to play in this aspect of the church's belief?

The answer to this illustrates a very important feature of doctrine-making in the church. As we have seen, official formulations of doctrine are dangerous things: they may result in some people being unable to assent to them and so feeling themselves excluded from the church. For this reason, churches are not usually in a hurry to define their doctrine; only some threat from outside – heresy, schism, state interference or the like – will force their hand. Throughout church history doctrine has tended to be made only when necessary: it has followed rather than preceded a crisis. Under normal circumstances Christian beliefs mature slowly; but at any moment a particular practical issue may force the church to make up its mind. And the result is – doctrine.

An excellent example of this was the debate from which my original quotation was taken. A request had been received from the Sikh community in Southampton to acquire a church which had recently been declared redundant. The decision lay with the Church Commissioners; but to assist them in making it, they asked for a debate to be held in General Synod on the principle involved, i.e. 'whether or not it is appropriate in certain circumstances for a redundant church to be made available for the worship of non-Christian faiths'. The debate duly took place in February 1983. Ten members of Synod made speeches, three of them laymen. All who took part were aware that, even if this were a question of principle, it was by no means academic or theoretical. A decision had to be made in Southampton one way or the other, and the course which would be taken by the Church Commissioners in the light of the debate could have important consequences, not just for relationships between the church and other religious bodies, but for race relations in general.

The arguments used on both sides of the debate ranged from the pragmatic to the theological. At a practical level, it was urged that new religious communities in British cities may be unable to rent or buy premises suitable for worship, mainly because they cannot obtain planning permission; that Christians have been greatly helped in the past by non-Christian governments overseas; and that making a church available would be a positive step in community relations. On the other hand, Christians had also received harsh treatment in Muslim countries; a church, once consecrated as a mosque or temple, would remain so (according to the laws of those religions) for the rest of time; and the effect on local residents (even some immigrants) of such a change of use would be confusing and even harmful. At a more philosophical level it was argued that to be denied a place to worship amounted to being denied a 'basic right of religious freedom' – and Christians must surely promote basic rights. On the other hand, all rights are limited by the rights of others, and it might not be proper for Christians in a Christian country to limit their own rights for the sake of others'. As for

theology, much play was made with Jesus' recorded
attitude to Samaritans and pagans, and there was
reference to official church documents which encourage
a positive attitude towards the social life and culture of
non-Christians. Many would have agreed with the view
of Professor Geoffrey Lampe, expressed ten years
previously, that 'the gospel is not commended by
hindering others from practising their religion'. But on
the other side there was concern for the evangelistic
edge of Christianity and the uniqueness of the Christian revelation. Would the sale of a church to Sikhs
imply that Sikhism and Christianity are 'viable alterna-
tives'?

Deep anxiety was felt, deep feelings were expressed.
The Christian instinct to serve, and to show every consideration for a neighbour in need, struggled against the
Christian imperative to preach the gospel in clear and
unambiguous terms. In the end Synod was fairly evenly
divided. The motion to make redundant churches available for this purpose was lost by a small margin. Evi-
dently the underlying questions are by no means resolved. A particular issue brought them to a head, and
forced the Church of England to declare its mind. But
its mind was not yet made up. The process of formulating belief on new issues, which we have been studying
in this book, had barely begun. In some form or other
the question will arise again. Some practical issue will
again precipitate the need to declare a doctrinal position. But by then, other things may have happened.
Theologians will have done some more work on the
theoretical background; more people will have been
involved in dialogues with other faiths; more Christians
may have had to confront questions of practical co-
operation with other religions over local issues, and to
work out their response to a new situation. Next time
round, Synod may be able to offer clearer advice. If

so, it will not be because – or only because – the theology of the question has received further study by experts. It will be because a larger number of church members have become involved in a complex and often demanding and costly process: that of finding a common mind through their Christian commitment, their reflection on their faith, their practical experience, their participation in worship and discussion, their ability to 'stand outside themselves a little' – in a word, their 'believing'.

9
Belonging

Thirty years ago the Archbishops of Canterbury and York were asked to address themselves to the question, What does it mean to belong to the Church of England? In reply, they drew up a document which may still be seen hanging in the porch of some parish churches: *A Short Guide to the Duties of Church Membership*. These 'duties' consisted entirely of personal obligations: regular attendance at services, particularly Holy Communion; regular prayer and Bible reading; the giving of service and money; and an exemplary manner of life.

In this book I have been asking the same question from a different point of view. I have asked how 'belonging' may affect, not so much the individual, as the church. I have suggested that, by virtue of belonging, a member of the Church of England may find himself involved in a variety of activities: joining groups for Bible study, taking responsibility for the conduct of worship and the choice of hymns, bringing his faith to bear on contemporary moral problems, ensuring that his local congregation is apprised of new thinking and new developments in his own field of secular life, becoming personally acquainted with adherents of other religions. Clearly these could hardly be called 'Duties of Church Membership'. It would be a remarkable church member who succeeded in doing them all; most of us could hardly manage more than one or two. They are not so much 'duties' as 'opportunities'. But I have argued that when 'belonging' to the church does take forms such as these, it affects, not just the health and vigour of the church (which it certainly does), but also the church's 'believing'.

Some may find this an exciting thought. The Church of England, they may feel, is getting out of date in a number of its beliefs: it is good to know that we can do something about it. But others may feel alarmed. Surely the church is not like a trades union or a political party, in which the activists can exert their influence and get the policy changed? Surely we are concerned with eternal truths? Surely Christian doctrine must remain, in all essentials, the same? Surely the Church is a place where sacred tradition is always more important than innovation?

This alarm would be justified, were it not that there is a large number of checks and balances which prevent the Church from making hasty and ill-considered changes in its belief. The Church is a stately ship. It may find itself in stormy waters, and may even have to undergo emergency repairs. But it has heeded the apostle's warning not to be 'tossed about by every wind of doctrine'. It has developed powerful instruments to ensure it remains on course. Before I finish I must re-assure those of my readers who are anxious about too much change, even though I must continue to encourage those who are ready to grasp their opportunities for contributing to the belief of the Church.

The first factor of real solidity is the central core of Christian doctrine itself. I have argued that it may never be possible to give a permanent and valid summary of Christian belief. Suppose one starts with a very basic statement of faith which in fact occurs in the New Testament, 'Jesus is Lord'. All Christians, surely, must assent to this. But they will not necessarily mean the same thing by it. 'Lordship' has very different connotations in different societies and cultures. In medieval England a 'lord' had considerable power over the entire lives of other people. In modern English, the word is used only of landlords and of peers of the realm, neither of whom can influence more than a small part of our daily activities. So what does it mean to confess Jesus as Lord? Still more questions arise from the statement, which is absolutely central to the Christian faith, that 'Jesus rose from the dead'. Again, one can hardly be a Christian at all without believing this. But what does it mean? Theologians offer a wide range of possible interpretations. Each of us probably has his or her own way of understanding it. We use the same form of words; but can we claim that we all have the same belief?

We saw earlier that one reason for these uncertainties is that the ultimate source of our knowledge of God and Christ is in Scripture, and that Scripture, for the most part, does not consist of doctrinal statements that could be valid for all time. Rather, it tells a story: the story of God's involvement with the world and his final self-revelation in the historical person of Jesus Christ. It is to this story that we must constantly refer when we seek to work out precisely what it is that we believe. Every Christian has a responsibility to engage in this quest; but we do not do it as if we were starting from scratch. What this story invites us to believe about God, Christ, the Holy Spirit, man and the world is a question which began to be answered within the New Testament itself. It was then strenuously pursued during the first Christian centuries, so that within five hundred years certain formulations were arrived at which commanded wide agreement at the time and have remained a point of reference for Christian belief ever since. We may not now be able to make these formulations our own. Each of us has still to work out the meaning the Christian story has for us in the language of our own time, and by so doing may make a contribution to the belief of the Church. But we have always to be sure that it is the same realities we are trying to express as those which caused our great predecessors to formulate Christian doctrine as they did. God, Christ, Spirit, creation, atonement – all of these we may one day have to find ways of making intelligible to ourselves and our friends. But this does not mean that we are free to jettison the reality behind any of them. In this sense, the Christian faith remains, and must always remain, the same. Each of us may have to find new ways of grasping these truths and making them meaningful to ourselves and others. But we do so within a community and a tradition which is utterly committed to the belief that the underlying truth can never change; for it is the truth of God.

Another factor which limits the influence of any individual or party within the Church is the cohesion of all the parts within the whole. I have been illustrating various ways in which church members may contribute to the forming of the Church's mind on a number of different issues. But it would be a mistake to think that any of these matters could be decided in isolation. Each of them is related to something else, and any new doctrine will have its effect on the whole fabric of Christian belief. Take once again the present debate over the ordination of women. It might be thought that this is a new issue. For various reasons the question of ordaining women to the priesthood has never before confronted the Church, and it can surely be discussed on its own merits, without affecting established church doctrines. But when one looks at the arguments used in the debate, one can see that what might have seemed to be simply a question of church order – whether or not to alter the law confining certain ministries to men – is in fact intimately related to other cherished beliefs. For example: some of those who argue against the ordination of women rely upon the clear statement of St Paul that women should be subordinate to men: 'the head of a woman is her husband' (1 Cor. 10.3). To the objection that what Paul says here was conditioned by the social

126

realities of his time and that he would have expressed himself differently in a society where the rights of women are acknowledged, they reply that this would be to undermine their confidence in the authority of Scripture. Paul's words mean what they say. To disregard their straightforward meaning would be to open the way to compromising with countless other texts of Scripture which happen to be inconvenient or unpopular today. For these people, therefore, the ordination of women cannot be considered without raising a very fundamental question indeed, namely the literal inerrancy of Scripture. It makes no difference that the majority of church members have a more 'liberal' approach to the interpretation of the Bible. Their own position is that the literal meaning must in all cases and wherever possible be obeyed; and the issue of the ordination of women cannot be considered in isolation from this basic doctrinal position.

Other opponents of the change argue from a quite different angle. For them, the distinctive role of the ordained minister is the celebration of Holy Communion. This has always been understood, in at least one tradition of Christian theology, as a kind of sacrifice. The minister is therefore a 'priest', and there is no warrant whatever in the Bible or the culture out of which it came for the introduction of a 'priestess'. For them, therefore, the issue again is not merely one of church order; it touches their deepest convictions about the nature of the Eucharist. To allow a woman to preside would be to rule out their traditional way of understanding the central act of Christian worship, and would therefore have profound implications for the entire structure of their faith.

If we examined the arguments of those who support the ordination of women we would find that the same is true. To say that times have changed and that new

127

social patterns justify new patterns of ministry implies a willingness to concede that many aspects of Christian belief and practice may have been a consequence of the social conditions of the time and can now be changed. Such a view would affect not only one's approach to the Bible, but also to the whole tradition of the Church. In short, this issue is as good an example as any of the principle that no question of Christian belief can be considered without reference to fundamental doctrine. Christian believing is not the adding together of many separate convictions; it means entering a system of beliefs such that any change at one point will have repercussions throughout the system. This is a factor which will inevitably make change a slow process. On the other hand, the system will have ceased to be alive if it has lost the ability to respond to new pressures exerted by its constituent parts.

Another constraint – though it may also be a stimulus – which affects the way in which the Church forms its belief is the ecumenical movement. This, again, is a relatively new factor. It was not until this century that churches felt obliged to do anything but maintain their own identity over against that of others. 'Boundary maintenance' was a high priority for all. But this has now changed. No church (in the West, at least) feels able to stand alone; and most now feel committed to observe a principle propounded by the World Council of Churches a few years ago: to do nothing separately which they are able to do together. That this is a factor which ought to influence decisions of individual churches has been frequently acknowledged in the debate on the ordination of women; it has been argued that to make this change would be to set back our relations with the Roman Catholic and Orthodox churches by many years. If this is so in this case, it must be so in others also; as a result, the freedom of one church to move in any direction, and consequently the freedom of church members to initiate any kind of change, seems to be seriously curtailed.

Is this really the case? It certainly is not how things have worked out in practice. The family of Christian churches ought not to be thought of as if it obeyed the rules of a military alliance. In NATO, it is true, no change of policy can be made without the prior agreement of all the allies. But in a family, one member can strike out on a path considerably different from that followed by the others. They may or may not follow him in the end – time will tell; but meanwhile they will continue to regard him as one of the family until and unless his chosen path leads him into a way of life that they recoil from themselves. If it does, they may have to disown him; but they will retain the family link as long as they possibly can. And so it is with the ecumenical 'family' of the churches. Individual members cannot wait for the whole family to agree before they make any change. The only change they must avoid is one that would put an intolerable strain on family loyalties. Some would say that the ordination of women would be a change of this kind; others that a move made by the Church of England (which would only be following the example of other provinces of the Anglican Communion) would be no more than another step along a road which all will have to follow in the end; family ties between the churches are surely strong enough to sustain the temporary tensions caused by being at different points along the road. In any case, what is required is not a refusal to move before all others have agreed, but a sensitivity to the difficulties which will be caused within a family when any particular move is made.

Constraints of this kind probably apply more to theologians than to ordinary church members. Indeed there are times when the ecumenical movement itself seems to be entirely in the hands of specialists. The obstacles to reunion seem to be in the realm of church order (mutual recognition of ministries etc.) or of traditional doctrines (the importance of the doctrine of justification by faith, or of transubstantiation). These are technical theological matters; and attempts to resolve them are slow and halting – the Church of England has had a particularly dismal record in this respect during the last few years. Fortunately, this is not the only level at which ecumenism is conducted. Up and down the country one can find members of all the major churches who meet regularly for common prayer, worship and study and who co-operate readily in matters of practical and social concern. Their frustration comes when they find that none of this cordial and often enthusiastic rapprochement at the local level seems to have any effect on the formal relationships of their churches. The experts at the negotiating tables seem to disagree as much as ever.

It may be useful to observe that part of the reason for this apparent paralysis may be that the process of 'believing in the church', which we have been describing in this book in specifically Church of England terms, is seen rather differently in other churches, and so causes difficulties when particular changes come to be debated. The best example is probably provided by the recent phase of discussions between the Anglican and Roman Catholic Churches ('ARCIC'). On the theological front, these discussions have been remarkably successful. Agreement was reached in less than ten years by those who made up the first International Commission on how to formulate the doctrines of the Eucharist, the Ministry, and the Church's authority. But on the last of these topics a difference began to emerge which may not be theological at all. It was agreed by all concerned that, in principle, a doctrine cannot be true merely because it is promulgated by the Pope and the Bishops under the assumed guidance of the Holy Spirit. To be received as certainly true, it must have also received the conscious assent of the lay members of the Church. For Anglicans, this is no problem. Every page of this book has been concerned, one way or another, with the way in which laymen take some responsibility, however small, for the belief of the Church of England and can therefore be assumed to be broadly in agreement with it. But in the Roman Catholic Church things are very different. The idea of a lay consensus is all right in theory; but there exist no means by which it can be established. There are few channels by which a lay voice may be heard or lay influence exerted. The kind of lay participation in the believing and decision-making of the Church which we have described in this book is impossible within present Roman Catholic structures. It follows that there is no prospect of agreement on this fundamental question of 'What makes doctrine true' until and unless the Roman Catholic Church takes into its system some of those procedures for lay participation which have been successfully established in the Church of England. It is here that ordinary church members have their opportunity. The more they can persuade their Roman Catholic friends of the part that can be played by laymen in testing and influencing the belief of the church, the sooner will unity be possible. In return, they will gain insight of other aspects of church life (such as the relation of personal spirituality to the regular worship of the church) in which the Church of England is particularly weak. Such is the arduous path towards unity. *Mutatis mutandis*, a similar process is involved in our relationship with the other major churches in this country.

We have now added a further trait to our imaginary portrait of the ideal member of the Church of England. Not only (in addition to all his church activities) should he become acquainted with other religions; he should also have discussions and share his experience with members of other denominations. But we still have not mentioned what is perhaps the most serious piece of discipline he must undertake before he can effectively contribute to the belief of the church. He must be ready to put every new formulation of doctrine, every new way of putting things, every proposal for a new style of Christian worship, witness or service, to the test of his own living, his own praying, his own conscience. This, indeed, is his main qualification for contributing at all. Christian doctrine is never merely passed down to the pews by academic theologians and church authorities. It is the result of a constant and complex dialogue between pew and pulpit, pupil and teacher, parish and diocese, layman and theologian, housewife and bishop ... the opportunities are endless, but they all presuppose that those taking part are committed to bringing their faith to bear on every aspect of their lives, and testing everything they receive from the church by their experience of witnessing to Christ in the world.

This means that the doctrine of the church – its belief, its teaching, its official formulations and forms of worship – can be true only if it 'works' in the experience of the church's members. A belief cannot be the church's belief if people find that they cannot believe it or put it into practice in any way. But different types of people can believe and do different things. It is here that perhaps we come closest to seeing how there may be such a thing as 'Church of England' doctrine. It is doctrine such as members of the Church of England have been able to assent to, have tested in their life of work, prayer and witness, and have found true to their experience. But what sort of people are these? Because of its particular history the Church of England includes a remarkably wide range of people. It includes (or at least refuses to exclude) those who come only for baptisms, marriages and funerals; those who 'don't like the new services' and stay away until a moment of crisis; those who appear only at Christmas, Good Friday or Easter; those who attend parish meetings only to protest; as well as all those who maintain their parish churches by hard personal work and sacrificial giving, who play their full part in worship and administration, who take responsibility for teaching the faith to children, and who serve the life of the church in countless (and often carefully concealed) ways. This is a wide spread. It includes men and women of every class, background and occupation (however poorly represented some may be in certain congregations). It is probably a more comprehensive and representative group of English people than can be found in any other church. The belief of the Church of England is a belief which is tested and endorsed by English men and women of every kind. It is a 'version' of Christianity whose truth rests on unusually broad credentials.

Yet all these people are English and, as such, are unlike people in other countries. An understanding of the faith which 'works' in this country may indeed be true and authentic, but it will not necessarily work elsewhere. To be a Christian in England in the nineteen eighties offers particular opportunities and imposes particular strains. A pluralist society, a liberal democracy, a welfare state, an acute class-consciousness, conspicuous wealth alongside relative poverty and real deprivation – these and many other factors constitute the environment in which an Englishman must work out his Christian values and priorities, his style of life and commitment to prayer, worship and service – in a word, his belief. The belief of the Church of England may reflect an unusually wide range of social and cultural backgrounds. But in other parts of the world Christians have to express their belief who are living in totally different circumstances. It is hardly to be expected that they will do so in exactly the same way as the members of the Church of England.

Consider, for example, the Roman Catholic Church in Poland. There, the main priority is simply survival in the face of a hostile and atheist government. For the Polish Christian, the circumstances of life are quite different from ours. Church members form the majority of the population; yet they are under constant threat from the regime. Evangelism, therefore, is not their main concern. What seems important is to maintain their traditional Christian style of life – their worship, their Christian education, their standards of personal morality and spirituality – and not to compromise in any way with the secular forces arrayed against them. As a result, the faith of their church seems, at least from the outside, to be exceedingly conservative. Their circumstances make any kind of change or innovation unwelcome. All their energies are devoted to holding on to the truth they have received. Their understanding of the Christian faith is one that certainly 'works' – for them; but it has now been left behind by that of more progressive parts of the Roman Catholic Church in other parts of the world.

Consider, by contrast, another area where the Roman Catholic Church is well represented: Latin America, the birth-place of 'Liberation Theology'. There, the great majority of church members are exceedingly poor, and living in conditions of flagrant oppression and injustice. No improvement seems possible by peaceful democratic means; but in present circumstances they are being denied the basic human rights and dignity which the Christian faith has always claimed for men and women of every race, nation and culture. In such conditions, how is the gospel to be understood and lived out?

Latin American theologians have proposed something new: Christian faith and witness demands the 'liberation' of the oppressed, even if this involves resorting to violence. Only so, in that situation, can practical expression be given to a living religion. The idea has caught on at other levels of the church. It is a 'version' of Christianity which has been found to 'work' in the particular circumstances of Latin America. Elsewhere, it has usually caused shock and dismay. How can the church deliberately promote violence? But we have been learning to respect the deep Christian dedication, as well as the practical involvement, of church leaders in those countries, some of whom have paid for their convictions by death. We are coming to recognize that some kind of 'liberation theology' expresses the authentic belief of the Latin American church. In their situation, it 'works'; it stands the test of experience and suffering as well as the scrutiny of the theologians who have to show its congruence with the historic Christian faith. But no one supposes that it will necessarily work elsewhere.

What then is the 'belief' of the Church of England? It is one that 'works' in the England of today. It is deeply marked by certain historical conditions which prevailed in the sixteenth and seventeenth centuries, and by the incomparable literary style of that period; but it has also submitted to a modernization of its thought and language which enables it to survive in the contemporary world. It is held and practised by people who are deeply conservative or radically progressive. It is shared by Catholics and Evangelicals. It continues to inspire social concern as well as attachment to the status quo. It is shared by young and old, simple and clever, rich and poor, weak and powerful. It is comprehensive and welcoming; often vague and non-committal, it is also often challenging. It enhances, without troubling, the security of countless bourgeois homes, yet it inspires lives of heroic service. Occasionally it is good news (to quote John Betjeman)

> . . . even to shining ones who dwell
> Safe in the Dorchester Hotel.

In short, it is profoundly English, with all the virtues and faults which that implies. But it is also profoundly Christian, and will remain so through all the insidious changes of our time, so long as those who 'believe' also 'belong' – belong in the full sense of working out within the church, in lives committed to worship, prayer and service, what it means to say: *We believe.*